Library
Research Guide
to
Religion and Theology
Second Edition, Revised

"Library Research Guides" Series

JAMES R. KENNEDY, JR. and
THOMAS G. KIRK, JR., Editors

Library Research Guide to Religion and Theology

Illustrated Search Strategy and Sources

Second Edition, Revised

by
JAMES R. KENNEDY, JR.
Reference Librarian
Earlham College

("Library Research Guides" Series, No. 1)

Pierian Press
ANN ARBOR, MICHIGAN

© 1984 by Pierian Press. All rights reserved
Published 1984
International Standard Book Number: 0-87650-185-4 (cloth)
0-87650-184-6 (paper)
Library of Congress Catalog Card Number: 84-61723

Pierian Press, Ann Arbor, Michigan
Printed in the United States of America

NOTE: Double hyphens have been used throughout the text
in place of dashes to indicate inclusive numberings.

Contents

Preface

Is This the Book You Need?

The answer is yes if you find yourself in one of the following situations:

1. If you are a *college junior or senior majoring in religion*, you will need to know how to locate appropriate library materials for term papers. This book assumes the card catalog and the *Readers' Guide* are "old friends," but you need to be introduced to the basic reference sources for religion. If, by some chance, you do *not* know how to use the card catalog and the *Readers' Guide* well, or have not written term papers for other courses that provided good library experience, then read the warning in the last two paragraphs of this preface.

2. If you are a *graduate student in religion*, perhaps a *seminarian*, you will be writing a number of research papers. This book will guide you to many useful reference sources.

3. If you are a *professor of religion* or a *reference librarian*, students often ask you for advice on how to find library materials for term papers in religion. It would be good to be able to recommend a library guide to these students. This is it.

Caveat Lector (Let the Reader Beware)

Do not begin with this book:

1. If you have somehow escaped learning how to use the card catalog and the *Reader's Guide*. Take the five-minute, self-graded test in Appendix 1, in case you wonder how much you know. If you fail the test, save this book until you have read the pages on the card catalog and the *Readers' Guide* in such books as: Margaret G. Cook, *The New Library Key*, 3rd ed. (New York: Wilson, 1975; or Jean Key Gates, *Guide to the Use of Libraries and Information Sources*, 5th ed. (New York: McGraw-Hill, 1983).

2. If you need to know the general procedures for writing term papers, including notetaking, outlining, and bibliographical forms. Use this book in conjunction with: Kate L. Turabian, *Students' Guide for Writing College Papers*, 2d ed., rev. (Chicago: University of Chicago Press, 1969); or Michael Meyer, *The Little Brown Guide to Writing Research Papers* (Boston: Little, Brown, 1982).

And Personally Speaking . . .

. . . while writing the first edition, I was a bit apprehensive about reviewers' reactions, because, so far as I knew, such a book had never been attempted. There were many books that described useful reference sources for a discipline, but none had ever focused on library search strategy. My twenty years' experience as a reference librarian convinced me that students needed to learn a systematic procedure for finding information on term paper topics, something they weren't getting from any of the available books. But is there a search strategy applicable for all topics and could I communicate it? I made the attempt and let the reviewers decide whether it was successful. Their response and that of the users was gratifying and caused the book to be reprinted several times.

Since that first edition, however, so many significant new reference works have appeared that I felt a new edition was needed. For example, *Old Testament Abstracts* and *Theological Dictionary of the Old Testament* are two major works that began after 1974. The intervening years have also seen the revision and updating of numerous works cited in the first edition. In addition, the development of computerized searching meant that the discussion of search strategy needed revision.

For all these reasons the author and the publisher have decided that a revised second edition is needed and would be worth the work. We hope you like this new effort.

Coach Vince Lombardi could not have won all those football games at Green Bay without plenty of help from his players, and this author could not have avoided a number of mistakes without plenty of coaching. Many thanks to Eleanor S. Bertelson, Thomas Blackburn, Sister Claudia Carlen, G. Fay Dickerson, Luella S. Eutsler, Evan Ira Farber, Kristine Huggins, Peter A. Johnson, Thomas G. Kirk, Victor L. Maxey, Mary Jo Peterschmidt Levy, John A. Petz, Robert Polzin, Tom Purdom, Carolyn Runge, John B. Trotti, Louis Voigt, C. Edward Wall and Glenn R. Wittig for all their comments on the next to last draft of the first edition. The author is also grateful to James R. Johnson and Margaret Karpe for their written suggestions for the second edition. Frederick C. Tiffany deserves special thanks for his advice on Appendix 2. Of course, none of the above professors, librarians, and students should be blamed for any faults in this revised edition. Someone has written that doctors can bury their mistakes and architects can cover theirs with ivy, but when an author puts a mistake in a book, brother, there it is, for all the world to see. If a reader sees something in these pages that needs fixing before the next edition, please feel free to write the author.

I would also like to express my thanks to Diana Battista and Robert Seitz, who did most of the typing, Edna Carter Southard, who helped with the final editing of the first edition, and Cameron Poulter, who designed the book.

I asked my wife, Laura, if she let me escape to do this writing because she wanted the world to be safe for term paper writers.

"No," she answered, laughing, "It was so you could express yourself and get your name on a title page."

Credits for Figures

Thanks are also due to the many publishers cited below who gave their permission to use excerpts from copyrighted works. Without their courtesy this book could not have been the illustrated guide that was intended. Uncopyrighted materials are also cited below in order to make the list of figures complete.

Figure 1: *The Interpreter's Dictionary of the Bible*. 4 vols. Copyright 1962 by Abingdon Press, vol. 3, p. 706.
Figure 2: Library of Congress catalog cards.

Figure 3: Metzger, Bruce M. *Index to Periodical Literature on Christ and the Gospels*. Grand Rapids, MI: Eerdmans, 1966, pp. xiii, xx, 505.
Figure 4: Strong, James. *The Exhaustive Concordance of the Bible* . . . . Nashville, TN: Abingdon, C1890, p. 991.
Figure 5: Macgregor, George Hogarth Carnaby. *The New Testament Basis of Pacifism and the Relevance of an Impossible Ideal*. New York: Fellowship Publications, 1960, p. 3.
Figure 6 and unnumbered figures: Hart, John. "B.C." comic strips. New York: Field Enterprises, 1971. By permission of John Hart and Field Enterprises, Inc.
Figure 7: Library of Congress, Subject Cataloging Division. *Library of Congress Subject Headings*. 9th ed. Washington, DC: Library of Congress, 1980, p. 1,720.
Figure 8: Library of Congress catalog cards.
Figure 9: Geldenhuys, Johannes Norval. *Commentary on the Gospel of Luke*. Grand Rapids, MI: Eerdmans, 1951, pp. 47, 570, 571, 572.
Figure 10: Orr, Edgar W. *Christian Pacifism*. Ashington, Rockford, Essex, England: Daniel, 1958, pp. 5, 167.
Figure 11: Eller, Vernard. *War and Peace from Genesis to Revelation: King Jesus' Manual of Arms for the 'Armless*. Scottdale, PA: Herald, 1981, p. 214.
Figure 12: *Essay and General Literature Index*. Copyright © 1970, 1971, 1972, 1973, 1974, 1975 by The H.W. Wilson Company. Material reproduced by permission of the publisher.
Figure 13: Reprinted by permission of the publisher from Robert Woito, *To End War: A New Approach to International Conflict*. Copyright © 1982 The Pilgrim Press.
Figure 14: Hershberger, Guy F. Review of Roland H. Bainton, *Christian Attitudes Toward War and Peace*. *Mennonite Quarterly Review* vol. 35 (1961), p. 324; and Lund, Doniver A. Review of Roland H. Bainton, *Christian Attitudes Toward War and Peace*. *Lutheran Quarterly*, vol. 13 (1961), pp. 184-85.
Figure 15: American Theological Library Association. *Index to Religious Periodical Literature*. "Book Reviews," vol. 5 (1960-62), p. 5 and "Periodicals Indexed."
Figure 16: *Book Review Digest*. New York: Wilson, 1963, pp. 988, 989; and *Book Review Digest, Cumulated Index, 1962-1966*. New York: Wilson, 1967, p. 615.
Figure 17: *Essay and General Literature Index, 1960-1964*. New York: Wilson, 1965, pp. 84, 1575.

Introduction

The Frustrations of a Term Paper

"A term paper will be due the last week of the course." If you are like most students, when you hear these words on the first day of class, you devoutly wish you had taken another course. It is not that you are a loafer. You just know from previous experience that, to get a decent grade on a term paper, you will have to cope once again with that monument to frustration: your college, university, or seminary library. Your memories of fishing for suitable library materials have given you some sympathy for Peter, when he fished all night without catching anything (Luke 5:5). Never yet have you managed to find those two essentials: a topic that really captured your interest and the books and articles that both stimulated and satisfied your curiosity about the topic. Sometimes you came close, but not without spending hour after frustrating hour thumbing through the card catalog and browsing in the stacks.

Our Purpose and Method

Your task may never be easy, but it will be much easier if you learn to use an effective search strategy and the appropriate reference sources. That is what this book is all about.

"But what is search strategy?" you ask. For our purposes search strategy may be briefly defined as a systematic way of finding an appropriate term-paper topic and then finding enough important library materials on that topic. As this book will show, search strategy involves much, much more than just looking up a few titles in the card catalog.

This book uses examples to teach basic search strategy and reference sources, which is not a bad plan if it is true that "the three best ways to teach are by example, by example, and by example." The primary example used throughout this book is a typical term-paper topic. The topic chosen is most relevant to Bible courses, but is also related to courses in church history and Christian ethics. Excerpts from the basic reference sources relate to the sample topic and demonstrate both search strategy and the use of these sources. This teaching method gives you a concrete demonstration which you can readily adapt to your own topic.

The Goal of This Book

Of course, learning takes time. As Mrs. Hoxie, the tennis coach, used to say, "The first 10,000 balls are the hardest." In learning the search strategy and reference sources for term papers in religion, only the first two are the hardest. After you write two term papers under the close guidance of this book, you will probably know what to do well enough to put the book aside, except for Appendix 2.

Then you can expect to see your former frustrations turn to joy. You will begin to look on future term-paper assignments as a welcome chance to pursue your own interests and perhaps be truly creative. Using this book can be the difference between term papers which are a labor of love and papers which are just plain labor.

John Hart, "B.C." comic strips. New York: Field Enterprises, 1971. By permission of John Hart and Field Enterprises, Inc.

1 Choosing Your Topic

I offer you the choice of life or death, blessing or curse. Choose life . . . Deut. 30:19 (New English Bible)

How to Begin to Choose a Topic

If you can choose your topic, choose a subject which really interests you. Such a topic will energize you, stir your imagination, and enliven your writing. Don't choose a topic just because it looks easy or because your professor seems to be interested in it.

Perhaps you choice of topic began months ago when you first read the Sermon on the Mount and were struck by Jesus' peace message. Perhaps you discussed pacifism with your pastor and were overwhelmed by the strength of his arguments against this position. Then you came across Gandhi's comment that he counted himself a follower of Christ, but that the so-called Christian nations had betrayed their Lord. They were more committed to violence and war than to love and peace. When you mentioned Gandhi's statement to your roommate, he reminded you that Jesus himself said, "I have not come to bring peace, but a sword." He even threw the moneychangers out of the temple.

So you are quite confused and yet very curious to know the truth regarding Jesus' teaching about peace. Such confusion and curiosity is the stuff from which term papers are made.

Perhaps you do not have a free choice of topic and are not intrigued by any of the possible topics before you. Let's say your professor in New Testament class has assigned the whole class to write on one of ten topics. None of the ten sounds exciting, but the one that seems least boring is "The New Testament and Peace." In this case, your first concern is to find some aspect of that topic which does arouse your curiosity.

At this point things are very much open-ended, with two broad terms (1) New Testament and (2) peace, that need, sooner or later, to be made more specific. For example, you could decide to narrow New Testament to Jesus Christ, and peace to pacifism. This would lead to "Jesus and Pacifism" as a preliminary working topic for the term paper. Chapter 2 of this book deals in greater depth with how to narrow the topic.

Why Look for Authoritative Summaries

In any case, your next step should be to find at least a couple of authoritative summary discussions of the key terms. Begin with the most specific term, "pacifism," and if this fails, try the broader term, "peace." Finding a helpful brief discussion of "Jesus Christ" may be a problem. He is so central to New Testament studies that you could be overwhelmed by the amount of reading. Perhaps you could find a useful article on an aspect of Jesus, such as his teaching or his ethic.

Are you wondering, why bother to look for summary discussions? Why not go straight to the card catalog, pick out a few books on your topic, and be done with your library research? This shortcut to library research is very popular among students, but it has serious limitations. When you base a term paper on a few randomly chosen books, you run the danger of uncritically repeating any biases or errors the writers may have. For instance, if you just happened to choose only books written by pacifists, your paper might totally overlook the alternative positions. Another weakness of the shortcut approach is that it tends to commit you too soon to a topic. It does not let you shop around.

Reading authoritative summary discussions of your topic will prevent the above problems and give you other benefits as well. Summaries allow you to survey the forest before you focus on a tree. They can give you a broad perspective and help you avoid the errors produced by a limited outlook. They can let you see how a subject has been subdivided, so that you can choose to focus on one of the subdivisions. If the summaries fail to stimulate your curiosity in the topic, then you can switch topics without much loss of time. The beauty of summaries is that they bestow all these benefits in very few minutes.

Where to Find Summaries

Summary discussions can be found in special encylopedias, in textbooks, in reserve books, and in other books your reference librarian can recommend. Probably the best place to look is in encyclopedias devoted to the subject you are studying. For a course on the Bible, the best encyclopedia is *The Interpreter's Dictionary of the Bible*, 4 vols. (New York: Abingdon, 1962). *Supplementary Volume*, 1976.[1]

----

[1]Encyclopedias for a number of other religion courses are cited in Appendix 2.

Don't be confused by the word "dictionary" in the title. This five-volume work contains encyclopedia-type essays, which are much more than the brief definitions found in most dictionaries. It was written by about 480 of the most capable biblical scholars in the world, including H.H. Rowley, Gerhard von Rad, and Oscar Cullmann.

The word "pacifism" does not appear in the Bible and has no entry in *The Interpreter's Dictionary of the Bible*. As shown in FIGURE 1, the *I.D.B.* does carry a one-page article, "Peace in the NT," which is signed by C.L. Mitton, a scholar identified in the front of volume one. Mitton helpfully discusses three meanings of peace, and one of these meanings, "peace as opposed to war or strife," bears directly on your tentative topic.

When using the *I.D.B.*, as well as any other books about the Bible, you will do well to note the most relevant verses of Scripture, because these can be used to locate a variety of invaluable writings that you would otherwise overlook. For instance, a single key verse of Scripture can lead you to extensive writings if you pursue it through Bible commentaries, periodical indexes, concordances, and other sources. We will be doing just that with the key verse, Matthew 10:34: "Do not think that I have come to bring peace on earth; I have not come to bring peace, but a sword." Later you will see how to locate this and other Bible verses by using a concordance. Mitton writes that Matthew 10:34 refers to "harmonious relations within the . . . family," which is not the interpretation your roommate suggested. Then you think of looking up the article on "sword" in *The Interpreter's Dictionary of the Bible* and discover that its author, J.W. Wevers, regards "sword" in Matthew 10:34 as "a symbol for war and dissension." He obviously disagrees with Mitton, but sees eye to eye with your roommate. You wonder what other scholars have written about Matthew 10:34, so you note Wevers's comment carefully for later reference.

Although the so-called "main line" Protestant scholars wrote most of the *I.D.B.*, students of all persuasions can benefit from their discussions of the Bible and its teachings. However, there are some doctrines, such as the doctrine of Scripture, on which conservative Protestants, sometimes called Evangelicals, do not agree with the main stream of Protestants. There are other doctrines, such as the doctrine of the church, on which Catholics differ with both "main line" Protestants and conservatives. Therefore conservative students should know about the following Bible dictionary written from a conservative perspective, which is half published: *International Standard Bible Encyclopedia*, ed. by Geoffrey W. Bromiley, fully revised. (Grand Rapids, MI: Eerdmans, 1979--). The first two volumes, published 1979 and 1982, cover letters "A" through "J." By the same token, Catholic students should be aware of the three-volume *Sacramentum Verbi; An Encyclopedia of Biblical Theology*, ed. by Johannes Baptist Bauer (New York: Herder and Herder, 1970). Besides the above multi-volume Bible dictionaries, students can benefit from a number of reliable one-volume Bible dictionaries, which are handier to use, but

PEACE IN THE NT [εἰρήνη]. In classical Greek the word is used to describe the cessation or absence of hostilities between rival groups. In the NT, however, the word carries a far wider range of meaning. This is partly because it was used in the context of Christian faith and experience, and partly because of the influence of the Hebrew word שלום. This word was represented in the LXX by εἰρήνη, and therefore its meaning dominates the Greek word which translated it. *See* PEACE IN THE OT.

The Hebrew word embraces all that the Gree^l word normally meant, and much more besi^d in the NT the Greek word has som^e of meaning of its Hebrew c^... ,3:11; should recognize this i^n ...m that peace 2:14; 19:42; Ro^... ...s the gift of Christ.

Becaus^e ...gnificance of the word, de- He^b ... ., there are, however, in the NT ,precise meanings which can be distin- ...d:

a) The first follows the usage of classical Greek and indicates peace, as opposed to war or strife. ← This is found in its ordinary secular sense in Luke 14:32; Acts 12:20. An extension of this meaning occurs in Eph. 2:14-17, where "peace" is the reconciliation which Christ has brought about between Jews and Gentiles, groups normally antagonistic to each other.

In I Cor. 7:15 it refers to "domestic peace" be- ← tween husband and wife, and in Matt. 10:34; Luke 12:51 to harmonious relationships within the whole family. In the sense of happy personal relationships

...and ...ates points to ...^i, it is difficult to deny ... 14:27, since the gift of peace is ...ed in contrast to the troubled and fear- ...arts of the disciples.

In certain contexts, therefore, "peace" may bear any one of these three distinguishable meanings. It is, however, more than probable that in many cases it is used comprehensively to embrace all three, as, e.g., when one Christian wished for another "peace from God." C. L. MITTON ←

FIGURE 1. The Interpreter's Dictionary of the Bible

which have fewer and shorter essays. Students in the "main line" Protestant tradition may, on certain points, prefer Frederick C. Grant and H.H. Rowley, *Dictionary of the Bible*, rev. ed. (New York: Scribner, 1963); conservative students may prefer James Dixon Douglas, ed., *The New Bible Dictionary*, 2nd ed. (Wheaton, IL: Tyndale, 1982); and Catholic students may prefer Xavier Leon-Dufour, *Dictionary of Biblical Theology*, 2nd ed. (London: Geoffrey Chapman, 1973), which actually has about twice as many articles as *Sacramentum Verbi*. But theological differences between biblical scholars are less and less important, as shown by the fact that the "main line" Protestant, conservative, and Catholic scholars are increasingly reading and learning from each other. You can follow their example by using several of the sources mentioned above.

The following religious encyclopedias have articles on many topics in religion, including the Bible's key words: *New Catholic Encyclopedia*, 15 vols. (New York: McGraw-Hill, 1967); James Hastings, ed., *Encyclopedia of Religion and Ethics*, 13 vols. (Edinburgh: Clark; New York: Scribner, 1908-27); *New Schaff-Herzog Encyclopedia of Religious Knowledge*, 13 vols. (New York: Funk & Wagnalls, 1908-12). It is important to note the date of publication in the above sources, as well as in other sources. The word "new" in the title of the *New Schaff Herzog* is now ludicrous because the work was published some seventy years ago. On the other hand, "new" is still an appropriate word to describe the *New Catholic Encyclopedia*. This was published about fifteen years ago and has been updated by two supplementary volumes, the latest published in 1979. This work shows the benefit of the truly revolutionary biblical scholarship during the past half century. *The Encyclopedia of Religion and Ethics* and the *New Schaff-Herzog Encyclopedia of Religious Knowledge* have articles useful to someone choosing a term-paper topic but they are simply too old to reflect the vast changes brought about by biblical archaeology, form criticism, demythologization and the like. The facts and interpretations in the older encyclopedias reflect the ignorance of their day.

Other Sources for Summary Discussions

This emphasis on religious encyclopedias is not meant to suggest that other special subject encyclopedias are not useful to religion majors. On the contrary, so many topics in religion are interdisciplinary that you will find yourself needing the encyclopedias as well as the periodical indexes and the bibliographies used primarily by students in other disciplines. For example, if you are writing a paper on religious art, you will benefit from using the *Encyclopedia of World Art* and the *Art Index*. If you are writing a paper for a philosophy of religion course, the *Encyclopedia of Philosophy* will probably be a big help. Of course, this handbook cannot present all other disciplines' reference sources in adequate detail. To do so would require a book many times this size. We can only stress that if your topic appears to be interdisciplinary, you should ask your reference librarian to introduce you to the realm of reference sources in the other discipline.

Textbooks and reserve books are another good place to find authoritative summary discussions of a topic. If your textbook does not provide an adequate summary for your tentatively chosen copic, try the books placed on reserve by your professor. He has put certain books on reserve because he regards them as authoritative and he hopes you will use them.

To locate other textbooks besides your own, look up your own textbook in the card catalog and note the subject heading or headings, called tracings, which are printed at the bottom of the card. Then these headings can be looked up in the card catalog in order to see what similar books the library owns.

As FIGURE 2 shows, if your textbook were *Understanding the New Testament*, by Kee, you would look at the

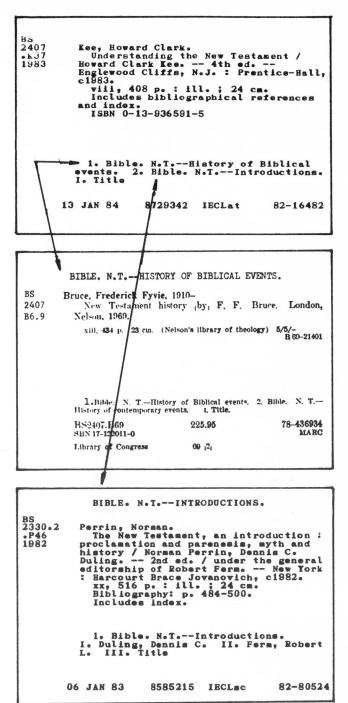

FIGURE 2. Catalog cards

bottom of the author card and note that the two subject headings assigned to it are: "Bible. N.T.—History of biblical events" and "Bible. N.T. — Introductions." As illustrated in FIGURE 2, when you look under these two headings, you might find, among others, Bruce's *New Testament History* and Perrin's *The New Testament*. If your textbook is not listed in the catalog, you may need to ask your reference librarian what its subject headings are.

Why Ask Your Reference Librarian

Maybe encyclopedias, textbooks, and reserve books will all fail to supply the needed summaries. Does this mean you should change topics? Not necessarily. First ask your reference librarian for help. A reference librarian's main job is to help students use the library effectively, but he or she is not a mind reader. So, if you have a problem, go to the reference desk. Ask your question as precisely as you can and tell the librarian where you have already looked. He may lead you to encyclopedias you never heard of, or he may show you particular subject headings in the card catalog. However, after some looking around, he may conclude that the library probably does not have the summary discussions you need. In fact, he may recommend that you change your topic because the library's resources appear to be too limited. It is better to change a dead-end topic early, before you have invested too much time in it. In any case, it is always wise to talk early and often with the term paper writer's best friend — a librarian.

Your professor is also a valuable resource person with whom to be in dialog at the beinning of your library search. He too can help you track down materials on a given topic.

Summary

1. Choose a topic which really interests you.
2. Begin your library search by reading summary discussions of your topic.
3. These summary discussions may be found in various encyclopedias or in textbooks, which can be located by identifying the subject heading assigned to your text.
4. Whenever you have difficulty, ask for help. The reference librarian is there primarily to help you.

John Hart, "B.C." comic strips. New York: Field Enterprises, 1971. By permission of John Hart and Field Enterprises, Inc.

Strait is the gate, and narrow is the way, which leadeth unto life, and few there be that find it. Matt. 7:14

Why Narrow Your Topic

While you may start your library search with a broad topic, such a topic must be brought within manageable limits, so that, unless your professor states otherwise, you end up writing on a topic that is fairly specific. There are several good reasons for this advice. First, you are only writing a term paper, not a book. Most topics as originally conceived by students are subjects on which whole books have been written. For example, a beginning opic, such as "Christian Teachings about Peace," is so big that it has been the subject of many books. Second, your time for reading is limited. The borader the topic, the more you must read before you can write. As you narrow your topic your required reading becomes less.

A third problem with term papers on broad topics is that they almost necessarily resemble the summary type of article found in encyclopedias. Generally, professors assign term papers so that you will study a limited area in some depth, not so that you will study a broad area superficially. If your paper starts to look like a mass of generalizations, take it as a sign that you need to narrow your topic and focus on specifics.

How to Narrow Your Topic

When you see that your original topic is much too broad, there are a number of library materials you can use to narrow it.

First, you can use the same encyclopedias, textbooks, and reserve books described earlier for their summaries and see how they subdivide your topic. One of the subdivisions may be an appropriate topic. For example, you would focus on "peace, as opposed to war," which *The Interpreter's Dictionary of the Bible* reported to be one of three meanings of the word "peace" in the New Testament, as was shown in FIGURE 1.

Second, you could use bibliographies, especially ones arranged by subject, in order to choose a viable subtopic. A good example is Bruce M. Metzger's *Index to Periodical Literature on Christ and the Gospels* (Grand Rapids, MI: Eerdmans, 1966). Metzger has indexed 160 periodicals from their beginnings to 1957. His bibliography, totaling 10,090 articles, is approached through a detailed table of contents, as illustrated in FIGURE 3. There is no separate

THEOLOGICAL STUDIES (505)

9254. Burton S. Easton, "The Ethic of Jesus in the New Testa-
" *ATR*, 14 (1932), 1-12.
" ustice in the Teaching of Jesus," *HJ*, 31

um." *NKZ*,

9266. Frederick C. Grant, "Ethics and Eschatology in the Teaching of Jesus," *JR*, 22 (1942), 359-370.
9267. Hillyer H. Straton, "Jesus, Exegesis, and War," *ATR*, 26 (1944), 42-48.
9268. Amos N. Wilder, "Equivalents of Natural Law in the Teaching of Jesus," *JR*, 26 (1946), 125-135.
9269. Johannes Herz, "Die sozial-ethische Gedankenwelt in Jesu Verkündigung," *TLZ*, 73 (1948), 747-752.
9270. Alfred M. Rehwinkel, "The Ethics of Jesus," *CTM*, 19 (1948), 172-189.
9271. Guy Martin Davis, Jr., "An Opinion Concerning the Pacifism of Jesus," *JBR*, 17 (1949), 181-186.
9272. Olof Linton, "I vad mån är Jesu etik eskatologiskt betingad?" *STK*, 25 (1949), 1-11.

XX — LIST OF PERIODICALS

FIGURE 3. Index to Periodical Literature on Christ and the Gospels

section for Jesus' teachings about peace; the section closest to the latter topic is entitled, "The Ethical Teaching of Jesus," on pages 503-6. Here, in chronological order, are included the citations for four articles on Jesus' teachings about peace, including item 9271, the one highlighted in FIGURE 3. (Finding only four articles is not very promising, but if none was found, perhaps the topic should be abandoned.) Note that item 9271 gives in order: the author, the title of the article, the abbreviation of the periodical, its volume number, date, and pagination. The "List of Periodicals" in the front of the volume decodes "JBR" in FIGURE 3 as the *Journal of Bible and Religion*.

Similar bibliographies for Paul's writings and for Acts are: Bruce M. Metzger, *Index to Periodical Literature on the Apostle Paul* (Grand Rapids, MI: Eerdmans, 1960) and A.J. Mattill and Nancy Beford Mattill, *A Classified Bibliography of Literature on the Acts of the Apostles* (Grand Rapids, MI: Eerdmans, 1966).

Third, you can use specific subdivisions in the card catalog. For example, the subject heading for "peace" is a very broad heading that, for the most part, includes books written by historians and political scientists. Much more precise and useful for our sample topic is the subdivision "Peace (Theology) – Biblical teaching." The fact that this heading exists is a good sign that you will be able to find enough materials to write a term paper on some aspect of it. How to arrive at this heading will be discussed in the next chapter.

Fourth, you can use Bible concordances. They refer to each passage where the principal words appear and also give part of the context. When your imaginary roommate (on page 3) quoted, "I have not come to bring peace, but a sword," he could not tell you where it came from, so that you could read it in context. The easiest way to locate this verse in a concordance is to look up either of its distinctive words, "peace" or "sword." "Sword" is faster because it appears less often in the New Testament. Take a look at FIGURE 4, the excerpt from James Strong, *The Exhaustive Concordance of the Bible . . .* (Nashville, TN: Abingdon, c1890). Note that the key word, "sword," is shortened to "s' " and that the verses are arranged in the same order in which they appear in the Bible. As FIGURE 4 shows, the beauty of a concordance is that by looking up "sword" you can not only find that your roommate was quoting Matthew 10:34, but you can also quickly spot the verse, "He that hath no sword, let him sell his cloak and buy one" (Luke 22:36). In contrast to these violent verses you can also find, "Put up again thy sword into his place, for all they that take the sword shall perish with the sword" (Matthew 26:52). Thus the concordance enables you not only to read part or all of a remembered verse but also to enlarge your understanding of key words by seeing them used in other verses and contexts. When you open your Bible to read the three verses cited above, you observe that they were all spoken by Jesus and you wonder how it is possible. Your curiosity, besides being thoroughly aroused, is more focused than before. You consider narrowing your topic to a study

FIGURE 4. James Strong, Exhaustive Concordance of the Bible

of Jesus' apparently contradictory sayings about swords.[2]

Of course, your use of relevant verses found in a concordance does not end when you look them up in a Bible and read the verses in their full context. Bible commentaries are arranged in scriptural order and periodical indexes and other sources have scriptural indexes, so that you can find what scholars have written about the particular passages you have found in a concordance, as will be shown in later examples. The more important and controversial the verse, the more material you are likely to discover.

Students of the original texts will find that the most useful concordance is Robert Young, *Analytical Concordance to the Bible . . .* , 22nd American ed. (New York: Funk & Wagnalls, 1955). After each of the key words in the

----

[2]This, in fact, will be the point around which the rest of our sample library search will center. The most fruitful examples will bear directly on that point. However, because it was difficult for the author to find an apt example in each reference source, some illustrations will deal with broader topics, such as "Jesus' Teachings about Peace."

King James version, Young gives the various Hebrew and Greek words that the English translates, both in their original characters and in transliteration.

The Interpreter's Dictionary of the Bible, as shown in FIGURE 1, also gives the original Greek and Hebrew, but does not report as many words as does Young. Knowing the Greek or Hebrew for a biblical word can be important because it allows you to discover the original meaning and not have to rely on a translator.

The only concordance to the King James version which includes the Apocrypha is one compiled by Alexander Cruden. The Revised Standard Version has its own computer-produced concordance: John W. Ellison, *Nelson's Complete Concordance of the Revised Standard Version Bible*. 2nd ed. (New York: Nelson, 1972). Concordances to other translations are cited in Appendix 2.

The fifth way to narrow a topic is to go to the shelves and examine the tables of contents and indexes of selected books found in the card catalog under the most relevant subject headings. For example, you could examine a few books under the heading "Peace (Theology) — Biblical teaching." You would look at the titles of chapters dealing with Jesus, the New Testament, or the Bible. FIGURE 5 shows that chapter 7 of Macgregor's book is entitled "Christ and Caesar," calling to mind Christ's words, "Render to Caesar the things that are Caesar's, and to God the things that are God's" (Mark 12:17). A study of this verse suggests that one way of narrowing an overly broad topic, such as "The New Testament and Peace," would be to write on the subtopic, "Christ's Message to the Christian Who is Facing the Draft."

You probably won't want to use all of the above five strategies to narrow your topic. All these ways are mentioned because, for a given topic, some ways will do the job and others will lead to dead ends.

CONTENTS

THE NEW TESTAMENT BASIS OF PACIFISM

THE RELEVANCE OF AN IMPOSSIBLE IDEAL

FIGURE 5. G. H. C. Macgregor, The New Testament Basis of Pacifism and the Relevance of an Impossible Ideal. New York: Fellowship Publications, 1960, p. 3.

Summary

1. It is vital to avoid writing on a topic that is too broad, because (a) you do not have time to write a book, (b) you do not have time to do extensive preparatory reading, and (c) you do not want to be superficial in covering a topic.
2. Narrow your topic as originally conceived by using any of the following: encyclopedias, textbooks, and reserve books; bibliographies; subject subdivisions in the card catalog; Bible concordances; and tables of contents and indexes of books.

And the Lord said, " . . . Come, let us go down, and there confuse their language, that they may not understand one another's speech." Gen. 11:6-7 (R.S.V.)

Limitations and Difficulties of the Card Catalog

You may recognize the card catalog as the most important single reference source in the temple of wisdom, but are you aware of its limitations? It indexes only the *general* subjects of *books*. It does not index parts of most books, nor does it provide access to periodical articles. And it does not give much help in evaluating the books it lists.[3]

A card catalog is usually simple to use if you need a particular book and know its author or title. You just look it up and copy its call number. The big difficulty with the card catalog comes when you try to find what books the library has on a particular subject. Then you must cope with the special language of subject headings, which is significantly different from spoken English.

----
[3]Chapter 5 suggests a tentative way to judge books according to the information on the catalog cards.

The Language of Subject Headings

The language of subject headings is arbitrary. For example, the phrase, "the biblical teaching about peace," is arbitrarily rendered as "Peace (Theology) – Biblical teaching" in the language of subject headings. It is not "Biblical teaching – Peace," "Biblical teaching about peace," or any other possibility that might occur to you.

You cannot count on logic to give you the correct subject heading. For instance, if you learn that the language of subject headings decrees the use of "Women in the Bible" and "Bible and science," you cannot deduce from these examples that "Peace in the Bible" or "Bible and peace" will be used. Despite the difficulty, making the effort to know the correct subject heading is essential. If you are to get the right response in your dialog with the catalog, you must communicate with it using its own vocabulary which, in this case is "Peace (Theology) – Biblical teaching."

FIGURE 6. John Hart, "B.C." comic strip. New York: Field Enterprises, 1971. By permission of John Hart and Field Enterprises, Inc.

Local librarians do not invent their own subject headings, but accept whatever headings are assigned to books by the nation's largest library, the Library of Congress. Fortunately the Library of Congress has published a dictionary that clarifies the language of subject headings, which is: Library of Congress, Subject Cataloging Division, *Library of Congress Subject Headings*, 9th ed., 2 vols. (Washington, DC: Library of Congress, 1980). These big red volumes and their paperback supplements are a complete guide to subject headings and their cross references used in the card catalog. These books are essential because subject headings, besides being arbitrarily chosen, are extremely numerous and often changed. Most libraries put "see" and "see also" cards in their catalogs as cross references, but they make only feeble attempts to keep up with the large number of additions and changes to subject headings. For this you need the subject heading books and their supplements though you may have trouble finding them. Some libraries do not put them out, because they were prepared primarily for catalogers and are hard for the average student to use without help. You may need to ask your reference librarian to get you the volumes and show you how to use them. If they are available, but are without any sign or person to teach you how to use them, study FIGURE 7.

FIGURE 7. *Library of Congress Subject Headings*, p. 1,720.

1. Headings in bold print are authorized for use, but your library is not likely to have any books under very specialized headings, such as "Peace Day."

2. Dashes indicate subject subdivisions. Under "Peace (Theology)" the most relevant subject subdivision for our purpose is "–Biblical teaching."

3. "*See*" references refer from unused headings to those which are used.

4. "*sa*," standing for "see also," refers to one or more related headings. The "see also" references under "Peace" which are most relevant to our need are "pacifism" and "pacifists." Twenty other "see also" references are also shown in the same column, but none is very relevant.

5. "*xx*," having almost the same meaning as "*sa*" directly above, refers to one or more related headings. "Ethics" and "War" are two "*xx*" references under "Peace" that will probably not help much in themselves because they are too general. However, by looking at the entries following "War," you will come to "War and religion," a heading that is highly relevant to your topic. By looking up "Pacifism," which was noted in the previous paragraph, you will find "*xx* Evil, Non-resistance to," which is definitely on target, because Jesus said, " . . . Resist not evil: but whosoever shall smite thee on thy cheek, turn to him the other also." Matthew 5:39. In the same way, you can expand your list of relevant subject headings by looking up any useful "*sa*" and "*xx*" references and by noting *their* "*sa*" and "*xx*" references, as well as their subject subdivisions.

1 → **Peace** *(International law, JX1901-1991)*
4 →   *sa* Arbitration, International
     Armies, Cost of
     Armistices
     Crimes against peace
     Disarmament
     International education
     International organization
     Islam and peace
     League of Nations
     Mediation, International
     Navies, Cost of
4 →   Pacifism
     Pacifists
     Peace treaties
     Peaceful change (International relations)
     Renunciation of war treaty, Paris, Aug. 27, 1928
     Security, International
     Sociology, Military
     War
     War, Cost of
     Women and peace
     World War, 1939-1945—Protest movements
     subdivision Peace *and* Protest movements *under names of wars*, *e.g.* World War, 1039-1945—Peace, World War, 1939-1945—Protest movements
5 →   *xx* Disarmament
     Ethics
     International relations
     Reconstruction (1914-1939)
     Security, International
     War
  Note under Pacifism
  — Biblical arguments
3 →   *See* Peace (Theology)—Biblical teaching
  — Societies, etc.
     sa subdivision Peace *and* Protest movements *under names of wars*, *e.g.* World War, 1939-1945—Peace; World War, 1939-1945—Protest movements
     x Peace movements
Peace, Bills of
   See Bills of peace
Peace, Breach of
   See Breach of the peace
Peace, Crimes against
   See Crimes against peace
Peace, Prayers for
   See Prayers for peace
Peace, Surety of the
   See Surety of the peace
Peace (Buddhism) *(BQ4570.P4)*
  xx Buddhist doctrines
Peace (Hinduism) *(BL1215.P4)*
  xx Hinduism
Peace (Jewish theology) *(BM538.P3)*
Peace (Philosophy)
  xx Philosophy
1 → **Peace (Theology)** *(BR115.P4)*
  xx Theology, Doctrinal
2 →   — Biblical teaching
     x Peace—Biblical arguments
  — History of doctrines
  — Prayer-books and devotions *(BT736.4)*
  — — English, [French, German, etc.]
3 → Peace and religion
   See Religion and peace
Peace and women
   See Women and peace
1 → **Peace Day** *(JX1936.5)*
  xx Holidays

To summarize the message of the symbols in the subject heading books, "sa" and "xx" references are authorized by the Library of Congress for use in the card catalog, but "x" references are not.

A basic rule in using subject headings is to look first under the subject headings that most precisely describe your topic; then, if you need more books, use broader or related headings. For example, the most precise headings for your paper on Jesus' teachings about the sword are "Peace (Theology) – Biblical teaching," "Jesus Christ – Teachings," "Swords (in religion, folklore, etc.)" and "War – Religious aspects." (Subject headings occasionally change, as reported in the supplements to *Library of Congress Subject Headings*. Before 1983 the last subject heading above was "War and religion.") The broader headings are "Peace," "Peace (Theology)," "Jesus Christ," and "Swords." The related headings include "Pacifism," "Nonviolence," "Evil, Nonresistance to," and "Christian ethics."

Finding the most precise subject headings under "Bible" is often a big problem because most card catalogs have hundreds of cards that begin with the subject heading, "Bible." Instead of thumbing through all those cards, you will save time by scanning the three pages of the subject heading books that list the subject subdivisions and their cross references. It will help to remember that "Commentaries," "Criticism, Interpretation, etc.," and "Theology" are standard subdivisions that are often used for individual books of the Bible as well as for the Bible as a whole. For example, the three most precise headings under "Bible" for a discussion of one of the key verses, Luke 22:36, are: "Bible. N.T. Luke – Commentaries;" "Bible. N.T. Luke – Criticism, interpretation, etc.;" and "Bible. N.T. Luke – Theology."

However, some libraries change the Library of Congress heading when it comes to "Bible. N.T. . . . ." Some simplify the matter by dropping "Bible" or "Bible. N.T." and use simply the book of the Bible, e.g., "Luke – Commentaries."

Most students are a little overconfident when using the card catalog. This is natural. After all, the card catalog has been your faithful guide for a long time. The above explanation is intended to be enlightening without giving a feeling of omniscience. Asking for guidance at the reference desk is generally advisable when coping with subject headings, because the correct subject headings can be so elusive. You can overlook them without knowing it and when this happens important books are missed. While subject headings may be the same in the card catalog as in periodical indexes, just as often these headings may be different. In using periodical indexes, a student will have to go through the same complex intellectual process to find the correct headings.

So be sure to ask your reference librarian to check your subject headings. It is as sensible and easy as asking the filling station attendant to check your oil. Since your reference librarian uses the card catalog regularly, he is knowledgeable about its special vocabulary and its idiosyncrasies.

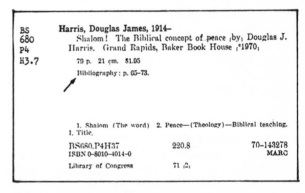

FIGURE 8. Catalog cards

These four cards illustrate points 1 to 5 above. Deems is an obscure author, W.B. Ketcham is not a prominent publisher, and the publication date is more than 90 years ago. In contrast, Oscar Cullman is a leading theologian, Harper & Row is widely respected, and 1970 is less than 15 years ago. The card for Harris's book includes mention of a nine-page bibliography, which may be more helpful to a student than the rest of the book. Kee's book is in its fourth edition, a sign that it has lasting value.

Judging Books from Their Catalog Cards

Of course, books listed under a given subject heading may differ widely in value. One of your tasks as a term-paper writer will be to find the better books and avoid the worse ones. How can you do this?

Although the card catalog itself does not evaluate books, you can make a preliminary and tentative judgment by using the following rough rules of thumb:

1. Date of publication

The most recent books are generally more desirable because their authors have had access to more accumulated knowledge, but this rule may vary greatly depending on the subject. For example, biblical and theological studies have developed so much in the last fifty years that it is wise to avoid most books in those fields that were published before 1930. Biblical archaeology, form criticism and Bultmann's demythologizing revolutionized biblical studies, while Barth, Brunner, Niebuhr, and Tillich revolutionized theology. The field of church history, meanwhile, has evolved more slowly, so that many older books are as useful as books published last year.

2. Author's authority

You may instantly recognize certain authors as being authorities, because your professors put one of their books on reserve or because you remember their names from one of the selective bibliographies.

3. Publisher's reputation

The major university presses, such as Oxford University Press, as well as independent publishers such as Harper and Row, Macmillan, Abingdon, Eerdmans and Sheed & Ward are among the publishers which can be trusted to publish worthwhile religious books.

4. Bibliographical note

A book with a bibliography will generally be more scholarly and useful than one published without a bibliography. In fact, you may benefit more from the bibliography in a book than from its text.

5. Edition number

Generally, a book has proved its value if it has been published as a revised, enlarged, or numbered (i.e., "fifth") edition.

NOTE: Obviously, the above five points, all illustrated in FIGURE 8, are so inconclusive that they emphasize one of the great limitations of the card catalog. It does not provide an effective way to evaluate books. Chapter 5 will describe better ways to make judgments about books.

The Computerized Catalog

As of 1984 only a small number of academic libraries have replaced their card catalogs with online catalogs that are accessible through computer terminals. However, many academic libraries are actively planning to switch to online catalogs within the next few years.

The online catalog has several advantages over the card catalog. Besides allowing for author, subject, and title searching, it also allows for searching individual words, publishers, and publication dates. It is also possible to show the relationships between words, using what is called Boolean logic. For example, the "and" command allows you to find all books in which the words "Peace" and "Bible" appear anywhere in the title or subject. The "or" command allows you to find all books in which the words "peace" or "pacifism" or "nonviolence" appear. Still another advantage of the online catalog is the possibility of examining the contents of other libraries. Libraries sometimes cooperate in setting up online catalogs and they share their cataloging information by computer.

Two cautions are in order when using an online catalog. First, you may be finding many books on your screen which are not in your library. If you do not have time to borrow books from other libraries, this is an important consideration. Second, your online catalog will not show "everything" in your library. It will show mainly books. It will not show periodical articles and is unlikely to show essays in books, both of which are essential to a thorough search.

Summary

1. The card catalog is limited because it indexes the *general* subjects of *books* only, and it does not evaluate them.
2. The language of subject headings is complex and arbitrary. The best guide to subject headings is *Library of Congress Subject Headings*. Subject headings preceded by "sa" and "xx" are authorized for use in the card catalog, but headings preceded by "x" are not.
3. Look first under the subject headings that most precisely describe your topic. Then use broader or related headings.
4. You can tentatively evaluate a book on the basis of its catalog card by noting the following: date of publication, author's authority, publisher's reputation, bibliographical note, and edition number.
5. If your library has an online catalog instead of a card catalog, then you will be able to search your collection more thoroughly — and you may also find what is in other libraries. However, not "everything" is listed in online catalogs.

And he shall separate them one from another, as a shepherd divideth his sheep from the goats. Matt. 25:32

A chapter, or part of a chapter, may be all you need from a book; yet it can be esential to your term paper. This is obviously the case when you are looking for interpretations of a particular biblical passage.

A Summary of Our Progress

To summarize our progress so far, the perplexing words, "I have not come to bring peace but a sword," led first to a concordance which identified the passage as Matthew 10:34. The concordance also served to recall Jesus' words, "He that hath no sword, let him sell his cloak and buy one," and identified this as Luke 22:36. Reading it in context showed that it is part of a dialog between Jesus and his disciples that extends from verse 35 to 38. To locate interpretations of Luke 22:35-38, the trail led next to the subject heading books, in order to determine the most useful headings in the card catalog. The precise heading for commentaries on Luke was shown to be "Bible. N.T. Luke – Commentaries." The subject heading books also showed there were several headings relevant to the topic of the passage, including "Peace (Theology) – Biblical teaching" and "War – Religious aspects." How to make a preliminary choice of the most promising books under a subject heading has also been shown.

Using Commentaries

The next step will be to go to the stacks and examine these commentaries. This should be easy because most will be shelved together, and arranged in scriptural order. Not all will be useful, however, because some will not comment on Luke 22:35-38. Those which do may be exceedingly enlightening because they bear so directly on the term-paper topic. It does not matter if only one or two pages are relevant as long as they serve your needs.

For example, Geldenhuys's *Commentary on the Gospel of Luke* gives two pages of verse-by-verse comment on the full passage, Luke 22:35-38. Especially significant is his view, which he shares with most scholars, that Jesus' "words in verse 36 should not be taken literally but in a figurative sense." But this is only the beginning! As FIGURE 9 shows, Geldenhuys also refers in a footnote to eight books that deal

THE TWO SWORDS

xxii. 35–8

35 And he said unto them,[1] When I sent you forth without purse, and wallet, and shoes, lacked ye anything? And they
36 said, Nothing. And he said unto them, But now, he that hath a purse, let him take it, and likewise a wallet: and he
37 that hath none, let him sell his cloke, and buy a sword.[2] For I say unto you, that this which is written must be fulfilled in me, And he was reckoned with transgressors: for[3] that which
38 concerneth me hath fulfilment. And they said,[4] Lord, behold, here are two swords.[5] And he said unto them, It is enough.[6]

ever cost with an unbreakable courage
that they will not relinquish the struggle.

38 The disciples are still blind to the spiritual nature of the Lord's work and kingdom. They are still hoping that He will establish an earthly Messianic kingdom with physical force. So they take the Saviour's words regarding the buying of a sword in a literal sense and do not understand their real meaning. In the light of the Saviour's other teachings (e.g. in the sermon on the mount) and of His perfect example, the disciples should never have taken those words literally. He does not rebuke them because they still have such a false notion of things that they could expect Him to be commanding armed violence, but ends the discussion sorrowfully. Later on during the night He forbade His disciples to use the sword, and by healing the wounded servant (verse 51) He taught them plainly and visibly that the use of the sword is not lawful in the defence of His cause. Therefore His words in verse 36 should not be taken literally but in a figurative sense.

COMMENTARY ON THE GOSPEL OF LUKE

Although a few, like J. Weiss and Goguel (*The Life of Jesus*, p. 454), declare that these words are intended literally, there is no doubt (in the light of Jesus' whole teaching and life) that the Lord intended them in a figurative sense. Most expositors are agreed on this point. Thus Dr. Luce declares: " Jesus' words are metaphorical and spoken with a sad irony " (*in loc.*). And Plummer: " Christ does not mean that they are to repel force by force; still less that they are to use force in spreading the Gospel. But in a figure likely to be remembered He warns them of the changed circumstances for which they must now be prepared ". V. Taylor, Lagrange, Easton, Zahn and others also take the words in a figurative sense. And T. W. Manson is right in stating: " The verse has nothing to say directly on the question whether armed resistance to injustice and evil is ever justifiable. It is simpl vivid pictorial way of describing the complete chan about in the temper and attitude of the disciples' min and

IX

BIBLIOGRAPHY

THE FOLLOWING are some of the more important commentaries on the Gospel of Luke:

J. Baljon, *Com. op het Evangelic van Lukas* (Utrecht, 1908).
H. Balmforth, *The Gospel According to St. Luke* (Oxford, 1930).
J. M. Creed, *The Gospel According to St. Luke* (Macmillan, 1942).
B. S. Easton, *The Gospel According to St. Luke* (T. & T. Clark, Edinburgh, 1926).
J. A. Findlay, *The Gospel According to St. Luke* (S.C.M. Press, 1937).
S. Greydanus, *Het Heilig Evangelic naar de Beschrijving van Lukas* (2 vols., Amsterdam, 1940).
A. J. Grieve, *St. Luke* in *Peake's Commen* 1936).
F. Godet, C

FIGURE 9. Johannes Norval Geldenhuys, Commentary on the Gospel of Luke. Grand Rapids, Mich.: Eerdmans, 1951, pp. 47, 570, 571, 572.

with the passage. Two of these are especially worth investigating, because they take the minority view that the words in verse 36 are "intended literally." However, a careless student could easily overlook the footnote and miss this bibliographical treasure. Or he might feel that the book is for scholars only and give up the search if he finds, as in FIGURE 9, that the footnote only mentions that there are works by V. Taylor, LaGrange, Easton, and Zahn, but does not give the authors' first names or the titles of their books. Instead, such partial references should lead one to look for Geldenhuys's bibliography, which cites all the works in full. FIGURE 9 demonstrates that a book such as Geldenhuys's can provide not only an invaluable two pages of comments, but also a selective bibliography leading to much further commentary.

Browsing the Stacks

Finding the useful pages in a commentary is easy compared with the process of browsing, which can also yield similar treasure. Even though browsing takes more time, it does uncover parts of books that are inaccessible through the card catalog or through bibliographies. Browsing works because library books are classified by subject in order to bring together on a shelf books that deal with the same topic. Similar books in the Dewey Decimal Classification will have the same numbers on the top line of the call number; in the Library of Congress Classification similar books will have the same top two and sometimes three lines.

To be an effective browser, begin with a cluster of the most precise subject headings on your topic and note the call numbers of the most promising books found under these headings. When you get to these books on the shelves, look not only at them but also at the other books with the same subject classification, as described in the previous paragraph. Be sure to examine the indexes in all these books, as well as their tables of contents. As shown in FIGURE 10, the table of contents in Orr's *Christian Pacifism* might cause you to stop after reading the chapters on Christ and the Gospels, pages 20 to 46, but the entry for "Jesus Christ" in the index leads to a number of additional pages, especially 47-62, 87-93, and 95-99. Of course, if a book has no index, then use its table of contents, even though it is not nearly as precise a guide as the index.

Browsing in the indexes of books less closely related to your topic can also enable you to discover relevant pages. For example, most books listed in the card catalog under "Jesus Christ — Teachings" will not have a whole chapter devoted to "Jesus' teachings about peace" listed in their table of contents. Any useful pages in these books can be found by exploring their indexes under "peace," "pacifism," "war," "nonresistance," "violence," and similar terms.

Also, many books about the Bible and about theology have a scriptural index, which can be used to locate writings on pertinent verses. As illustrated in FIGURE 11, the "Index of Scripture Cited" in Eller's *War and Peace from Genesis to Revelation* provides a quick way to discover that Matthew 10:34-39 is discussed on pages 151-152.

Contents

INDEX

FIGURE 10. Edgar W. Orr, Christian Pacifism. Ashington, Rockford, Essex, England: Daniel, 1958, pp. 5, 167.

NEW TESTAMENT

FIGURE 11. Vernard Eller. *War and Peace from Genesis to Revelation*. Scottdale, Pa.: Herald, 1981, p. 214.

Another way to locate parts of books is to use two continuing reference works that index collections of essays: *Religion Index Two* and *Essay and General Literature Index*. Far more widely available and of much longer time span is the *Essay and General Literature Index, 1900–1933*, edited by M.E. Sears and M. Shaw (New York: Wilson, 1934) and its *Supplements* (New York: Wilson, 1937). This index comes out semiannually, with annual and five-year cumulations. It provides the easiest way to locate essays and miscellaneous articles which have appeared in collections but which have been buried in the card catalog under broad subject headings that do not indicate whether a collection includes any essays on your precise topic. The five-year volumes enable you to search through the eighty-three years of material covered by the index in a matter of minutes. The *Essay and General Literature Index* does not duplicate what you will find in subject bibliographies because the latter rarely cite individual essays or articles.

Using this index takes three steps. If you are looking for recent writings on peace by religious leaders, you will find much under the subject, "peace." (Most subject headings in the *Essay and General Literature Index* are identical to the ones you used in the card catalog.) As shown in FIGURE 12, it cites an essay, "Explorations in Gandhi's Theory of Nonviolence," by K.H. Potter. Note the information following the italicized "In." Second, look up this information in the "List of Books Indexed" in the back of the volumes under whatever word follows "In." This gives the full bibliographic information about the book. Third, look up that book in your card catalog to see if your library owns it.

It is unfortunate that *Religion Index Two; Multi-Author Works, 1970–1975; 1976–* (Chicago: American Theological Library Association, 1978–) is not more widely available in libraries. This annual is comparable in purpose to *Essay and General Literature Index*. Both provide subject and author indexes to collections of essays, but the great value of *Religion Index Two* for religion students is that *all* its collections are in the field of religion, whereas *Essay and General Literature Index* devotes most of its coverage to other disciplines. The subject headings for *Religion Index Two* are the same as those for *Religion Index One* and, like *Religion Index One*, it has both an author index and a subject index.

As this chapter has shown, parts of books which are relevant to a topic can be found by using Bible commentaries, by browsing, and by using the *Essay and General Literature Index* and *Religion Index Two*. If these sources were *not* used, important pages would be missed.

Summary

1. A chapter or a few pages may be all you need from a book. You can find a page or more that interpret a biblical passage by looking in commentaries, which are arranged in scriptural order.
2. Browsing will uncover useful pages that are inaccessible through the card catalog or through bibliographies. Browsing involves examining books which are shelved next to the promising books you found through the card catalog. Use their tables of contents and indexes; pay attention to their footnotes and bibliographies.
3. The *Essay and General Literature Index* and *Religion Index Two* are used to locate essays and miscellaneous articles, most of which would otherwise have remained buried in the card catalog under broad subject headings.

ESSAY AND GENERAL LITERATURE INDEX, 1970-1974

Nonviolence
King, M. L. Pilgrimage to nonviolence; excerpt from "Stride toward freedom"
In What country have I? p112-16
Potter, K. H. Explorations in Gandhi's theory of nonviolence
In Power, P. F. ed. The meanings of Gandhi p91-117
Zinn, H. The force of nonviolence
In Rose, T. ed. Violence in America p14-25
See also Passive resistance

Moral and religious aspects
Curtis, C. J. The Negro contribution to American theology: King
In Curtis, C. J. Contemporary Protestant thought p197-209
Nonviolent noncooperation. See Passive resistance

LIST OF BOOKS INDEXED

Powell, Lawrence C.—*Continued*
Southwest classics; the creative literature of the arid lands. Essays on the books and their writers. Ward Ritchie Press 1974
ISBN 0378-07751-1
LC 73-89437
See also entry under title: Stuart and Georgian moments
Power, Paul F.
(ed.) The meanings of Ghandi. Univ. Press of Hawaii 1971
ISBN 0-8248-0104-0
LC 72-170180
"An East-West Center book"
Power and community. See Green, P. and Levinson, S. eds.
Power & consciousness. See Cruise O'Brien, C. and Vanech, W. D. eds.

FIGURE 12. *Essay and General Literature Index.* Copyright © 1970, 1971, 1972, 1973, 1974, 1975 by The H. W. Wilson Company. Material reproduced by permission of the publisher.

5   Evaluating Books

Judge not according to the appearance, but judge righteous judgment.   John 7:24

Why Some Library Books Are Not Trustworthy

Some books are truly superb — as Milton wrote, "the precious life-blood of a master spirit." Others are so bad that hardly anyone should read them. Of course, most books fall between these extremes. Librarians try to select the most worthy books, but they will occasionally buy inaccurate, biased books or accept them as gifts. Most librarians believe that a wide spectrum of views should be represented on their shelves, so that students can be exposed to them. Sometimes a librarian will buy any English language book on a given topic, especially a popular, new topic, just to meet the demand. All this adds up to another *caveat lector* (let the reader beware): Do not trust a book just because it is in the library.

Evaluate extremely carefully any book or books on which you are basing your term paper. For example, if your paper stands or falls on the reliability of the facts and interpretations in G.H.E. Macgregor's *The New Testament Basis of Pacifism* (1936) you want to be as certain as you can be that his book is trustworthy. You want to know if other scholars supported, questioned, or rejected his ideas.

Don't judge a book by its cover, and, as was stressed in chapter 3, don't judge a book only from its catalog card either. This is why bibliographies and book reviews are so indispensable.

Selective Bibliographies

A book can probably be trusted if it appears on an authoritative, selective bibliography in the field. A good example is the one excerpted from *To End War* and shown in FIGURE 13. This bibliography, found in the card catalog under the subject heading "Peace — Bibliography," has several characteristics which make it almost ideal for a student writing a paper on Jesus' teachings about peace. First, it is authoritative, having been selected and criticized by a number of scholars, as described in its preface. Second, it is selective. It lists only fourteen of the most important books under "Ethics and World Politics: Why Mass Violence Is Never Justified — Pacifism," whereas a really comprehensive bibliography would list hundreds. Third, it is arranged by subject, and the subject mentioned above is close to our concern. Fourth, it has annotations which describe the books

> **Q. Ethics and World Politics: Why Mass Violence Is Never Justified— Pacifism**
>
> 15– 151 *The New Testament Basis of Pacifism*, G.H.C. MacGregor, 160pp, 1968, Fellowship, O.P. A classic statement based on a careful analysis of the New Testament. Sees the obligation to accept suffering as the basis of Christian nonviolence.
>
> 15– 152 *The Dagger and the Cross*, Culbert Rutenber, 138pp, 1965, Fellowship, O.P. A careful survey of the Biblical foundations of pacifism written in the context of contemporary Christian thought.
>
> ...ny.
>
> ., a Historical and Theological
> .. of Peace Witness and Church-State Rela-
> . .pp, 1968, Herald, $1.50. A summary of the content and a
> ...ceological exposition.
>
> 15– 159 *New Call to Peacemaking, A Challenge to All Friends*, Norval Hadley (ed.), 80pp, 1976, Faith and Life, $1.00. Seven authors seek to re-establish and clarify the Friends commitment to nonviolence, and to then go about building the conditions of peace in world politics.
>
> 15– 160 *New Call to Peacemakers*, Maynard Shelly, 96pp, 1979, Faith & Life, $2.00. A wide-ranging work calling Christians to simpler lifestyles, to recognition of their "violence" in sustaining U.S. corporations who are accused of exploiting others. The definition of "violence" employed is so broad that it is doubtful if anyone can be nonviolent.

FIGURE 13. Reprinted by permission of the publisher from Robert Woito, *To End War: A New Approach to International Conflict*. Copyright © 1982 The Pilgrim Press.

more fully than do their titles. For example, it helps to know that *New Call to Peacemakers* is "calling Christians . . . to recognition of their 'violence' in sustaining U.S. corporations who are accused of exploiting others." Fifth, it is up-to-date, having been published in 1982.

It is worth hunting for such a bibliography because it can save you time in your search and allow you to proceed more confidently. This bibliography provides the basic reading, but of course it would need to be supplemented by commentaries, articles, book reviews, and other bibliographies found in all these sources.

Book Reviews

When it comes to evaluating a book, book reviews are far more helpful than selective bibliographies. The scholars who review books are often as great or even greater authorities on a subject than are the authors of the books they are reviewing. These scholars may question or reject certain facts or ideas they find in a book that is central to your paper. As you read the book, you may have wondered about these facts or ideas yourself, but since you are only an embryonic scholar in that field, you did not feel qualified to do more than wonder. In this case, your best strategy is to read book reviews.

Of course, not all reviewers will agree on the evaluation of a book. Their disagreement will lead you to viewpoints you might otherwise have missed. FIGURE 14 illustrates a basic disagreement between reviewers of the same book, *Christian Attitudes Toward War and Peace* by Roland H. Bainton. Hershberger wrote, "The historical survey is excellent . . . ," whereas Lund wrote, "In the area of recent history there are so many errors and distortions that this reviewer is moved to despair." Who is to say who is right? You are! This is a call to further reading and reflection as well as consultation with your professor.

When reviewers disagree among themselves, you must think for yourself. Paul said to "work out your own salvation with fear and trembling" (Phil. 2:12). If you would "work out your own" evaluation *without* "fear and trembling," then share your thinking with your professor.

Reviews may also strengthen your bibliography because

As Da....
there are grounds for .....
"But if not" (that is, if in spite of ...
perative another World War does break forth), ...
three Hebrew youths, "be it known unto thee, O king, that ...
serve thy gods, nor worship the golden image which thou hast set up. (266)

→ The historical survey is excellent, the writing carries the sprightly pungent style which we have come to expect from Bainton, and the scholarship is of a high order. The book also carries the inevitable Bainton illustrations, many of them cartoons. In a few cases, however, sweeping generalizations and striking figures of speech, while making for a story well-told, also lead to exaggeration, misleading interpretations, or even violence to facts. For example, the statement that the Mennonites agreed with the argument of Celsus that the Christian must either go to war or retire to the desert, that " the only valid pacifism is monasticism," (252) is carrying a point just a little too far. Neither is it true that the Pennsylvania Mennonites refused to vote. It may also be noted that the American Peace Society was organized in 1828, not 1838. The Second Hague Conference was held in 1907, not 1906.

Goshen College   GUY F. HERSHBERGER

ters ⌐
standards ⌐
volume. The list
loaded with cartoons ⌐
disillusionment and catastro⌐
war, none to show the tragedy o⌐
and oppression.

→ In the area of recent history there are so many errors and distortions that this reviewer is moved to despair. On page 200 the claim that "Spain had conceded our demands" in 1898 is open to question; it is patently false that "President McKinley declared war." On page 214 Professor Bainton refers to a four-power treaty which was quite different from the one he describes. Whereas present historians of American diplomacy (Bemis and Bailey) refer to the treaties of this Washington Conference as "a face saving retreat" and judge that the "achievements . . . proved to be temporary and somewhat illusory," Professor Bainton states that the "United States gained heavily." On political and military events Professor Bainton relies heavily on documents which fit his case, takes too little account of the more reputable sources. His analysis of positions taken by churchmen and organized churches represents a real contribution.

I am glad that this book was written. It is a part of the growing body of literature on Christian responsibility. It sharpens the edge of debate. It presents a clear testimony by a mature religious scholar of a major problem of our times.

DONIVER A. LUND

FIGURE 14. Guy F. Hershberger, review of Roland H. Bainton, Christian Attitudes Toward War and Peace. Mennonite Quarterly Review, vol. 35 (1961), p. 324; and Doniver A. Lund, review of Roland H. Bainton, Christian Attitudes Toward War and Peace. Lutheran Quarterly, vol. 13 (1961), pp. 184-85.

reviewers often compare a new book with other books in the field. Reviews are not the first or second place to look for bibliography, but it is good to be alert for such references when reading reviews.

Indexes to Book Reviews

Because a review could appear in so many different issues of so many different periodicals, finding a review of a particular book might seem like hunting for the proverbial needle in the haystack. Fortunately it is more like looking up a number in the phone book. Most reviews that you will need can be located easily through an index to book reviews.

The most useful index to book reviews in religion is published in the last fourth of each volume of *Religion Index One: Periodicals; A Subject Index to Periodical Literature, Including an Author Index with Abstracts and a Book Review Index.* (Chicago: American Theological Association, 1949-- .) This growing index, which is primarily an index to articles in religion, now covers over 300 scholarly, religion periodicals, but when it began in 1949 (with the title *Index to Religious Periodical Literature*) it covered only thirty-one. Most are Protestant in orientation; a few are Jewish and Roman Catholic; and the great majority are in English.

Cited in FIGURE 15 are nine reviews of Bainton's book from periodicals and reviewers which represent a wide range of theological perspectives. *Brethren Life* and *Mennonite Quarterly Review* are published by two of the historic peace churches, whereas *Lutheran Quarterly* represents a denomination that has regularly opposed pacifism as a theological stance. John M. Swomley, Jr., who is shown to have written one review, is an eminent spokesman for pacifism, whereas John Coleman Bennett, another reviewer, is well known for his sober arguments against the pacifist position.

You can look up the abbreviations of periodical titles in "Periodicals Indexed," which is just inside the front cover of each volume. An excerpt is shown in FIGURE 15.

Two other periodical indexes are especially helpful in locating reviews in theological periodicals. *Catholic Periodical and Literature Index* (Haverford, PA: Catholic Library Association, 1930--) covers over 130 Catholic periodicals and is primarily an index to their articles, but it also cites book reviews in the backs of volumes. *C.P.L.I.* will be discussed in chapter 6, along with other periodical indexes. *Book Reviews of the Month, An Index to Reviews Appearing in Selected Theological Journals* (Fort Worth, TX: Fleming Library, Southwestern Baptist Theological Seminary, 1962--) is a monthly index to about 180 periodicals and is arranged by subject according to the Dewey Decimal Classification.

In addition to the three specialized indexes mentioned above, you can find reviews through three general indexes to book reviews. *Book Review Digest* (New York: Wilson, 1905--), although it covers only eighty-two periodicals, has four advantages: it has been published since 1905; it carries excerpts of the reviews; it reports the length of the full

review; and up until 1972 it has indexes that cumulate five years in one alphabet. Besides covering six religion periodicals, *America, Christian Century, Christianity Today, Commonweal, Journal of Religion,* and *Journal of the American Academy of Religion*, it also indexes some religious book reviews written by leading theologians in general periodicals, such as *The New York Times Book Review*.

As FIGURE 16A shows, the 1962 to 1966 cumulative index to subjects and titles of book reviews lists three books reviewed under the subject heading, "War and religion." This is the same subject heading used in the card catalog before 1983, as reported in Chapter 3. This index can also be examined for the other subject headings authorized for use in the card catalog, whether or not any books were found under those headings. The arrow in FIGURE 16A shows that Ramsey's *War and the Christian Conscience* can be looked up under both its subject headings and its title. The notation "(My '62)" indicates that fuller information is available in the 1962 annual volume of *Book Review Digest* and that the book originally appeared in the May issue.

Arranged alphabetically by author, *Book Review Digest* cites twelve reviews of Ramsey's book and gives excerpts from seven of these. In the example in FIGURE 16B, three reviews are mixed, as shown by the "+--," and three are favorable, as shown by the "+." (*Book Review Digest* stopped using + and -- in 1963.)

The excerpts give a good idea of the main thrust of the reviews, but you may want to read the complete review.

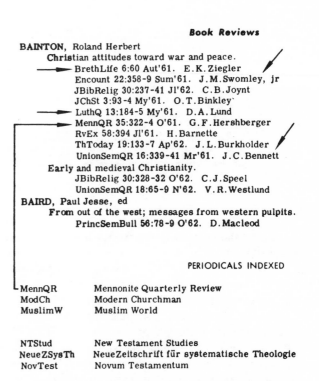

FIGURE 15. Index to Religious Periodical Literature

War and religion
Keys, D., ed. God and the H-bomb. (Ag '62)
Lawler, J. G. Nuclear war. (Mr '66)
Ramsey, P. War and the Christian conscience. (My '62)
War and revolution. Timasheff, N. S. (Ag '66)
War and the Christian conscience. Ramsey, P. (My '62)
War crime trial, Nuremberg. See Nuremberg Trial of Major German War Criminals, 1945-1946

FIGURE 16A. Book Review Digest, Cumulated Index

FIGURE 16B. Book Review Digest

RAMSEY, PAUL. War and the Christian conscience; how shall modern war be conducted justly? pub. for the Lilly endowment res. program in Christianity and politics. 331p $6 Duke univ. press
261.6 War and religion   61-10666
"The author, a professor of religion at Princeton, considers theories of the 'just war,' the use of unlimited means, and the nature of rational armament." (Foreign Affairs) Bibliographical footnotes. Index. This volume represents an extension and an elaboration of a series of three lectures delivered by Professor Ramsey at Duke University.

"The most recent study published for the Lilly Endowment Research Program in Christianity and Politics, this book deserves the respectful attention of those involved in nuclear statecraft and of all students of ethics and war." P. F. Power
+ Am Pol Sci R 55:927 D '61 800w
Reviewed by G. F. Hershberger
Ann Am Acad 344:144 N '62 550w
"Presentation is forbiddingly difficult for the average reader."
Booklist 58:297 Ja 15 '62
"In spite of much that is excellent the book contains certain obvious weaknesses. From the standpoint of ethical theory, the author's doctrine of the 'just war' smacks of formalism. . . . Again, it is extremely doubtful that Ramsey has proved his thesis; namely, that the 'just war' doctrine—even his revise version—is relevant to the nuclear age. . . . Finally, by virtually condemning them to political ineffectiveness Ramsey has not been fair to Christian pacifists. . . . In spite of these strictures, I consider this book worth reading. Above all else it will cause both pacifists and nonpacifists to re-examine their foundations. It might even have a good effect on those militarists who take the time to read it." A. W. Munk
+ — Christian Century 78:957 Ag 9 '61 1250w
"Ramsey . . . argues for limited war fought within the bounds of the traditional just war doctrine. . . . Ramsey, one of the most distinguished contemporary Protestant theologians . . . is extremely strict in his insistence on the distinction between combatants and noncombatants, which he formulates in terms of

counter-force and counter-people war. . . . Ramsey would start now, unilaterally if necessary, to bring our means of defense down to the levels where they can be used for counter-force warfare. . . . But, supposing . . . that the United States is in fact moving away from preparations for counter-people war, the problem still remains: What adequate answer would there be to nuclear, counter-people blackmail if the willingness or capacity to retaliate in kind were absent? We need further thinking here; and it is to be hoped it will attain the levels of scholarship and moral perception which characterize Dr. Ramsey's incisive work." W. V. O'Brien
+ — Commonweal 74:521 S 22 '61 750w
Ethics 72:76 O '61 40w
Foreign Affairs 40:143 O '61 40w
"Confronted with the hugeness of nuclear weapons, the World Council of Churches Commission felt compelled to abandon the 'just war' category of thought altogether. Professor Ramsey, who draws together the threads of Protestant and Catholic thought on this matter in a way too seldom attempted, criticises this approach strongly. . . . He seeks to make a case . . . for 'counter-forces' warfare, even with nuclear weapons, as 'just' and feasible, compared with the total unacceptability of 'counter-peoples' warfare, whatever the weapons employed. . . . Professor Ramsey's book is, I suppose, too much a collation of other men's minds to be called great. But it is originally conceived, trenchantly executed, and above all timely." Christopher Driver
+ Guardian p7 N 3 '61 900w
Reviewed by R. L. Short
+ Hibbert J 60:79 O '61 60w
"Ramsey is one of America's most prominent scholars in the field of Christian ethics. His subject is an important one. It is disappointing that it is not treated lucidly enough to have substantial appeal for the general reader. For libraries with unlimited budgets." R. W. Schwarz
Library J 86:2806 S 1 '61 130w
"It is an informed and reasonably balanced treatment with a considerable amount of moral wisdom. In the specific applications that are made to particular strategic and tactical problems it seems, however, to go rather too far." W. G. Pollard
+ — N Y Times Bk R p3 Ja 28 '62 90w
Reviewed by R. M. Brown
Sat R 45:24 Ap 21 '62 70w

RAND, ANN. Edward and the horse [by] Ann Rand and Olle Eksell. unp il $3 Harcourt

For example, the reviewer in the excerpt from the *Christian Century* states that "it is extremely doubtful that Ramsey has proved his thesis," but the reviewer's case is not spelled out in the excerpt, which is only about 120 words. Much more is available in the full review as indicated by "1250 w," meaning 1250 words, following the citation of the source. In contrast, the review in *The New York Times Book Review* is only ninety words long and more than a third of it is quoted. The shorter the review the less likelihood that you will want to take time to dig up the complete review.

Essay and General Literature Index helps locate critiques of major publications, such as Augustine's *The City of God*. Augustine brought the concept of the "just war" into Christianity. Since *Essay and General Literature Index* only indexes essays and miscellaneous articles in books rather than periodicals, this index cites discussions that tend to be much longer than the average review in a journal. It is one of the handiest places to look for critiques of books published before *Book Review Digest* was started in 1905.

Essay and General Literature Index was shown in FIGURE 12 as an index to essays in books. To find an essay review, as illustrated in FIGURE 17, you would look first under the author's name, Augustine, where you would find a *see* reference from Augustine to Augustinus, which is his last name in Latin. Then look under the title of the work, *The City of God*, which is always in italics and centered in the column.

If you wanted to read Riley's "Ecclesiastical Morals: St. Augustine (354-430 A.D.)," you would look on pages 165-79 of *Men and Morals* by I.W. Riley. The "List of Books indexed" in the back of *Essay and General Literature Index* gives full bibliographic information on Riley's book. Your card catalog will tell whether it is in your library.

The other easy place to look for critiques of books published before (as well as after) 1905 is in the card catalog under the author's name as a subject. For example, many books about Augustine include discussions of *The City of God*.

As FIGURE 18 shows, Battenhouse's book, along with others, appears in the card catalog under "Augustine." It has an index so that you can quickly find the precise pages dealing with *The City of God*, as well as Augustine's concept of war. You can also use the card catalog and indexes in books, in the same way shown in Chapter 4, in order to locate critiques of books by leading contemporary theologians such as Reinhold Niebuhr and Rudolf Bultmann.

If the book you want to see reviewed is related to one of the so-called secular disciplines, it may well be reviewed in the professional journals of that discipline. Many of these disciplines have their own special indexes to book reviews, comparable in importance to *Religion Index One: Periodicals*. For example, Peter Mayer's *The Pacifist Conscience* (1966) is reviewed in philosophy journals indexed in the *Philosopher's Index*. To discover the indexes to reviews in other disciplines, consult your information specialist, the reference librarian. Such indexes are too specialized for this guide, but your reference librarian will know which ones you need.

If all else fails, your reference librarian may give you a list of your library's holdings of religious periodicals. If the list includes periodicals dealing with the general subject of the book you want to see reviewed, you can go directly to the periodicals themselves.

Augustinus, Aurelius, Saint, Bp. of Hippo
—About—*Continued*
Harnack, A. von. The world-historical position of Augustine as teacher of the Church
In Anderson, Q. and Mazzeo, J. A. eds. The proper study p247-54
Jaspers, K. Augustine   ustine:
In Jaspers, K. The great
    p175-229   great psycholo-
McNamee, M. B   .stotle to Freud p82-
Augusti
In M
About Individual works
The city of God
Mommsen, T. E. Orosius and Augustine
In Mommsen, T. E. Medieval and Renaissance studies p325-48
Mommsen, T. E. St Augustine and the Christian idea of progress: the background of The city of God
In Journal of the History of Ideas. Ideas in cultural perspective p515-43
In Mommsen, T. E. Medieval and Renaissance studies p265-98
Riley, I. W. Ecclesiastical morals: St Augustine (354-430 A.D.)
(In) Riley, I. W. Men and morals p165-79

Confessions

LIST OF BOOKS INDEXED

Riesman, David, 1909-
    Abundance for what? And other essays. Doubleday 1964
    Individualism reconsidered, and other essays. Free Press [1964 c1954] (Free Press paperback)
Right reason in the English Renaissance. See Hoopes, R.
Riley, Isaac Woodbridge
    Men and morals; the story of ethics. Ungar 1960
The rise of English literary prose.

FIGURE 17. Essay and General Literature Index

Cicero, 24, 36, 59, 94, 142, 275; *Hortensius*, 23, 97, 373
Circumcellions, 70, 77, 179, 192
City of God, occasion and theme, 51-3; surveyed, 257-81

W

Watkin, E. I., 411, 415
War, view of, 42, 82; *justa bella*, 272
Warfield, B. B., 230
Wesley, John, 60

BR 1720 A9 B3.3   AUGUSTINE, AURELIUS, SAINT, BISHOP OF HIPPO.
Battenhouse, Roy Wesley, 1912-   *ed.*
    A companion to the study of St. Augustine. New York, Oxford University Press, 1955.
    425 p. 22 cm.

1 Augustinus, Aurelius, Saint, Bp. of Hippo.   I. Title.

BR1720.A9B33   281.4   55—6253 ‡
Library of Congress   [56x10]

FIGURE 18. Roy Wesley Battenhouse, ed. A Companion to the Study of St. Augustine. New York: Oxford University Press, 1955, pp. 419, 425.

INDEX.

IS BIBLICAL SCHOLARSHIP ENOUGH?

THE NEW TESTAMENT BASIS OF PACIFISM. By G. H. C. MacGregor. London, James Clarke & Co., 1936. $1.20.

Reviewed by Leonard S. Kenworthy

I had just finished reading William W. Cadbury's thought-provoking article, "The War, Seen from Canton," when I spied G. H. C. MacGregor's book on my desk, waiting to be reviewed. Here, I thought, I will find a partial answer to the dilemma that confronts the pacifist in the distraught world which William Cadbury has brought so close in his article in THE FRIEND. The jacket further encouraged me by stating that the author of *The New Testament Basis of Pacifism* h~ ~ clared himself a pacifist "no~ ~ ~ountries political grounds, b~~ ~ ~ ~vations of words. New Test~~ ~ ~s, sometimes as many as ten

Here I found a cold, theological discussion of pacifism rather than an answer to my desire for a warm, radiant application of Christ's teachings and life to our modern world. The author, of course, cannot be blamed for this disappointment. He did not write the book to answer the question which I had wanted answered. But he did, I presume, write the book to fortify the pacifistic convictions of some and to persuade others to accept similar views. There is little chance that such an intention will be fulfilled in this little volume. It is too scholarly and scholarship will not suffice here. To the theologian concerned with Biblical interpretation the book may be satisfying, but hardly to the layman.

Yet, the author's conclusions are worth mentioning even if you do not read the entire book. First of all he asserts that the teachings and practice of Christ were "unequivocally pacifist" and

FIGURE 19. The Friend

For example, you would look for a review of Macgregor's *The New Testament Basis of Pacifism* in *The Friend*, because it is a publication of the Society of Friends, one of the historic peace churches. Like most periodicals, *The Friend* has its own index, as shown in FIGURE 19, which may be bound into the front or back of the volume. This index collects reviews under the heading, "Book Reviews," but other indexes collect them under "Reviews" or "Criticism." Sometimes an index does not collect reviews but lists them under author and/or title.

Because scholarly journals publish reviews up to four years after their year of publication, you may need to look in several volumes before you locate a review.

Note the author's criticism in FIGURE 19, which contrasts with the favorable annotation Macgregor's book received when it appeared in the selective bibliography shown in FIGURE 13.

The last paragraph of the review in *The Friend*, which is not shown in full in FIGURE 19, provides a helpful summary.

Biographical Information to Judge an Author's Competence

All is not lost if your reference librarian cannot find a review of a book that is central to your paper. You can often get a good idea about an author's competence by finding a review of another book by the same author. Another strategy is to find biographical information that indicates whether the author of your book is considered an authority in his field. His occupation, education, and publications are all ways to measure his authority.

In considering an author's occupation, notice his field of endeavor (whether it is religion or another field), along with the status of his place of employment, and his rank. (The pecking order in higher education is: professor, associate professor, assistant professor, and instructor.) To illustrate all these variables at once, a book on Jesus is probably more reliable if it is written by a full professor of New Testament at Harvard Divinity School than if it is written by an instructor of speech at a junior college. However, this way of evaluating a person is sometimes dead wrong. How ironic that Nathanael should be referring to Jesus when he asked, "Can anything good come out of Nazareth?" (John 1:46. R.S.V.).

An author's other publications can be evaluated in terms of their quantity, quality, and subject matter. An author is more likely to be trustworthy if he has published several other books in the subject area, especially if they have been favorably reviewed. Beware of the author whose only other publication was in an altogether different field.

Five Sources of Biographical Information

You do not have to rely on prayer or good luck in order to locate the kind of biographical data described above. Of course, you may have the good luck to find a biographical blurb from a dust jacket pasted into the front of a book by your author. If you find no such blurb, do not despair. Simply look up your author in one or more of the following reference sources:

1. *Who's Who in America* (Chicago: Marquis-Who's Who, 1899--) is a biennial that presents in condensed form the basic biographical data on about seventy-five thousand living American V.I.P.'s in all fields, including Robert F. Drinan, the author of *Vietnam and Armageddon; Peace, War, and the Christian Conscience.*

Drinan's claim to fame as a man of many talents is supported by the presence of his name in this reference work. Note in FIGURE 20 that three inches of small type report the highlights of his education (LL.B, 1949; Th.D., 1954), his work (Dean of the Boston College Law School 1956--70 and member of the 92d-96th Congresses from Massachusetts), his memberships (Association of American Law Schools), and his publications (four books and articles in journals of opinion).

Living Americans of slightly lesser importance appear in the regional biographical handbooks, *Who's Who in the East, Who's Who in the Midwest, Who's Who in the South, Who's Who in the West*, and *Who's Who in the South and Southwest*. The data on deceased Americans who formerly appeared in *Who's Who in America* are collected in *Who Was Who in America*, which has seven volumes covering 1906-1981. An index volume covers all seven volumes.

2. *Who's Who* (New York: St. Martin's Press, 1849--) is published annually and carries data on important living Britons. It has the same format as *Who's Who in America* and is the British equivalent. Britons who are deceased appear in *Who Was Who*, which has seven volumes covering 1897-1980.

3. *Directory of American Scholars*, 8th ed. (New York: Bowker Company, 1982) is a four-volume work. The most useful volume for religion majors is volume 4, which carries Who's-Who type data on about 7,800 American and Canadian scholars in the fields of religion, philosophy, and law. If your author does not appear in volume 4, try the index to all four volumes which is at the back of volume 4.

If you were looking up Edward LeRoy Long, the author of *War and Conscience in America*, you would not find him in *Who's Who in America*. However, you would find in the

DRINAN, ROBERT FREDERICK, lawyer, Congressman, educator, clergyman; b. Boston, Nov. 15, 1920; s. James Joseph and Ann Mary (Flanagan) D.; A.B., Boston Coll., 1942, M.A., 1947; LL.B., Georgetown U., 1949, LL.M., 1950; Th.D., Gregorian U., Rome, 1954; study, Florence, Italy, 1954-55; LL.D., Worcester State Coll., 1970, L.I. U., 1970, R.I. Coll., 1971, St. Joseph's Coll., Phila., 1975, Syracuse U., 1977, Framingham (Mass.) State Coll., 1978, U. Santa Clara, 1980, Kenyon Coll., 1981, Lowell U., 1981, U. Bridgeport, 1981, Loyola U., Chgo., 1981, Gonzaga U., 1981. Entered S.J., 1942, ordained priest Roman Cath. Ch., 1953. Admitted to D.C. bar, 1950, Mass. bar, 1956, U.S. Supreme Ct. bar, 1955; asst. dean Boston Coll. Law Sch., 1955-56, dean, 1956-70; vis. prof. U. Tex. Law Sch., 1966-67; mem. 92d-96th congresses from 4th Dist. Mass.; mem. jud. com., govt. ops. com., house select com. on aging, chmn. subcom. on criminal justice; columnist Nat. Cath. Reporter, 1980; prof. Law Center, Georgetown U., Washington 1981--. Chmn. adv. com. Mass. U.S. Commn. Civil Rights, 1962-70; mem. vis. com. Div. Sch., Harvard U., 1975-78; bd. dirs. Bread for the World; founder Nat. Interreligious Task Force on Soviet Jewry. Mem. exec. com. Assn. Am. Law Schs. Fellow Am. Acad. Arts and Scis.; mem. Am., Mass. (v.p. 1961), Boston bar assns., Am. Law Inst., Ams. for Democratic Action (v.p., pres. 1981--), NCCJ (nat. trustee), Common Cause (nat. governing bd. 1981--). Author: Religion, the Courts and Public Policy, 1963; Democracy, Dissent and Disorder, 1969; Vietnam and Armageddon, 1970; Honor the Promise, America's Commitment to Israel, 1977. Editor: The Right To Be Educated, 1968; editor-in-chief Family Law Quar., 1967-70; corr. editor America, nat. Cath. weekly, 1958-70. Contbr. articles to jours. of opinion. Office: Georgetown U Law Center 600 New Jersey Ave NW Washington DC 20001

FIGURE 20. Copyright © 1982, Marquis Who's Who, Inc. Reprinted by permission from *Who's Who in America*, 42nd Edition.

LONG, EDWARD LEROY, JR, b Saratoga Springs, NY, Mar 4, 24; m 82; c 3. RELIGION. *Educ:* Rensselaer Polytech Inst, BCE, 45; Union Theol Sem, BD, 48; Columbia Univ, PhD, 51. *Hon Degrees:* LHD, Maryville Col, 80. *Prof Exp:* Instr physics, Rensselaer Polytech Inst, 45; assoc prof philos & ethics, Va Polytech Inst, 51-54 & philos & relig, 55-57; from assoc prof to prof relig, Oberlin Col, 57-76; PROF CHRISTIAN ETHICS & THEOL OF CULTURE, THEOL & GRAD SCHS, DREW UNIV, 76- *Concurrent Pos:* Minister, Blacksburg Presby Church, Va, 51-54; mem summer session fac, Union Theol Sem, NY, 56, 67 & 71; Soc Relig Higher Educ fel, 57; lectr, Oberlin Grad Sch Theol, 58-59; Guggenheim fel, 63; Caldwell lectr, Louisville Presby Sem, spring 69; fel law, ethics & relig, Harvard Law Sch, 69-70; Soc Relig Higher Educ fel cross disciplinary studies, 69-70; advan pastoral studies, San Francisco Theol Sem, 72; Danforth Found Underwood fel, 73 & 74-75; mem, Coun Studies Relig, 73-76; Eli Lilly vis prof sci, theol, human values, Purdue Univ, fall 75; vis prof Christian ethics, Gen Theol Sem, 77-78; lectr Christian ethics, Union Theol Sem, 78-79; lectr, Princeton Theol Soc, 80-81. *Mem:* Am Acad Relig; Am Soc Christian Ethics (vpres, 71, pres, 72-73); Am Soc Polit & Legal Philos; So-Sci Studies Relig; Am Theol Soc. *Res:* Theological ethics; ethics of pedagogy and governance in higher education; the relationships of science, theology and culture. *Publ:* Auth, The Role of the Self in Conflicts and Struggle, Westminster, 63; A Survey of Christian Ethics, Oxford Univ, 67; Soteriological implications of norm and context, In: Norm and Context in Christian Ethics, Scribner, 68; War and Conscience in America, Westminster, 68; A content analysis of study materials in the campus ministries, In: The Church, the University and Social Policy, Wesleyan Univ, 69; co-ed, Theology and CHurch in Times of Change: Essays in Honor of John Coleman Bennett, Westminster, 70; auth, US vs the Harrisburg Eight: Conspiracy Prosecution for Illegal Dissent, Dert Church &

FIGURE 21. *Directory of American Scholars*. 8th ed. New York: R.R. Bowker (a Xerox company), 1982. p. 322.

Directory of American Scholars, as FIGURE 21 shows, that he does have significant credentials. The excerpt reports that he earned a Ph.D. from Columbia University in 1951, has been a professor of Christian Ethics at Drew University since 1976, and was president of the American Society of Christian Ethics, 1972-1973.

4. *Contemporary Authors: A Bio-Bibliographical Guide to Current Authors and Their Works* (Detroit, MI: Gale, 1962--). This continuing series of volumes gives biographical and bibliographical data on some seventy thousand authors. To find which of more than forty volumes describes an author, use the cumulated index found at the back of alternate volumes. *Contemporary Authors* often provides fuller information than is available in *Who's Who in America* or the *Directory of American Scholars*. For example, Roland H. Bainton, the author of *Christian Attitudes Toward War and Peace*, received twenty-four inches in *Contemporary*

Authors, compared with two inches in *Who's Who in America*. Additional features of *Contemporary Authors* are its report of "Work in Progress," references to more biographical information, and "Sidelights," which includes opinions, hobbies, and other activities. Much of the data has been updated in the New Revision Series of *Contemporary Authors*, but much is still not "contemporary." Therefore students will need to use the other sources listed in this chapter, in order to get current information.

5. *Biography Index* (New York: Wilson, 1946--) is a quarterly index to biographical articles appearing in books of collective biography, as well as in some fifteen hundred periodicals. It also cites complete books about a person. The index itself only identifies people in terms of their dates, occupations, and nationalities. When no nationality is reported, the person is a U.S. citizen. Annual and triennial cumulations make this source handy to use.

As FIGURE 22 shows, the cumulation for 1961 to 1964 cites four kinds of biographical publications about the author of *Christian Attitudes Toward War and Peace*: a yearbook, a chapter in a book, a periodical article, and a bibliography in a book. This example is not typical of the quantity of information available, because most religious leaders are not as distinguished as Roland Bainton.

Biography and Genealogy Master Index, 2nd ed., 8 vols. (Detroit: Gale Research, 1980), along with its three-volume *Supplement* published in 1982, indexes over four million biographical sketches appearing in more than 350 biographical sources, including titles such as *Contemporary Authors* and *Dictionary of American Biography*. If you are not finding someone quickly, this would be faster than *Biography Index*, because, *Biography and Genealogy Master Index*, along with its 1983 supplement, has only two alphabets to examine, whereas *Biography Index* has twelve. *Biography and Genealogical Index* is more expensive than *Biography Index* and is not as widely available.

In Case of Failure with All the above Sources

If all the above biographical sources fail you, it is not time to give up. It is time to see your reference librarian. She or he will probably be able to suggest other sources that might be successful.

Some photocopy machines have the following sign for people who would rather use intuition than common sense: "If everything else fails, read the instructions." When it comes to evaluating a book central to your term paper, if the previous advice fails, think for yourself and consult your professor. Have *you* noticed errors or omissions in the book? Does it run counter to what *you* have understood to be true, on the basis of your other reading and what you have heard in class? Does it seem to *you* to be biased in any direction? But before you commit yourself to a position, it is wise to discuss your conclusions and uncertainties with your professor. You will get a better education if you change your

views while in the process of writing a paper than if you change your views afterward because your paper came back with adverse comment. Change is a little late then. Of course, such consultation requires getting an early start on a paper. You do not want to be so rushed at the end that you must skip this important step.

Other Uses for Biographical Sources

Evaluating books is not the only use for the biographical sources described in this chapter. You can also use them to get better acquainted with your professor and to pursue topics in church history. For example, a student working on the history of alternative service programs for conscientious objectors would find help not only under the subject heading, "conscientious objectors," but also under "Jones, Rufus," because this Quaker was a prime mover in setting up these programs. Finding biographical materials on Rufus Jones would call for use of *Biography Index* and the card catalog, as a start.

```
BAINTON, Edgar Leslie, 1880-1956. Australian
    composer
  Bainton, Helen. Remembered on waking:
    Edgar L. Bainton. Currawong '60 117p il
BAINTON, Roland Herbert, 1894-  church his-
    torian
  Biography
→  Cur Biog por 23:6-8 Je '62
   Cur Biog Yrbk por 1962:20-3 '63
→ Harkness, Georgia. Roland H. Bainton; a
    biog. appreciation. (In Littell, Franklin
    Hamlin, ed. Reformation studies. John Knox
    press '62 p 11-18)
→ Lost leaders. por Time 80:42 Jl 13 '62
   Bibliography
→ Morris, Raymond P. Bibliography of Profes-
    sor Bainton's writings on the reformation
    period. (In Littell, Franklin Hamlin, ed.
    Reformation studies. John Knox press '62
    p251-3)
BAIRD, Albert Craig, 1883-  speech educator
  Hitchcock, O. A. Albert Craig Baird. (In
```

FIGURE 22. Biography Index

Summary

1. Do *not* trust a book just because it is in the library.
2. A book is probably trustworthy if it appears on a selective bibliography.
3. The most helpful evaluation of a book generally comes from book reviews. The three major indexes to reviews in religion periodicals are *Religion Index One: Periodicals, Catholic Periodical and Literature Index*, and *Book Reviews of the Month*. Also useful are *Book Review Digest*, which indexes reviews in periodicals of general interest, and *Essay and General Literature Index*, which indexes critiques in books.
4. Biographical information about an author can help to establish whether he is an authority. Five reference sources are recommended for locating this information.
5. You can also use biography sources to find out about your professors and to pursue topics in church history.

Why Periodical Articles Are Important

When "liberation theology" became prominent around 1973, one could not study it simply by reading the books by its leading proponents, such as Gustavo Gutierrez. One had also to read the theologians who debated against the "liberation theology" theologians, and their arguments appeared in periodicals long before they appeared in books.

The debate on Christian attitudes toward war and peace, while not as new and volatile as the debate on the "liberation theology," is nevertheless a subject of continuing controversy. There has been no final peace declared between the Christian apologists for war under certain conditions and Christian pacifists who declare that all wars are unchristian. Roland Bainton's book, *Christian Attitudes Toward War and Peace*, has traced this debate up to 1960, and later books, such as Thomas A. Shannon's *War or Peace?: The Search for New Answers* (1980), have updated the debate. However, the latest word is not found in books, because of the lag in their being published. A book manuscript may be two or more years old before its publication date, whereas the time elapsed between the writing of a periodical article and the date of its publication may be only a few months or even weeks.

In other courses in religion you will have greater need for periodical articles than you will in biblical studies. In applied Christian ethics, for example, you need the latest thinking about the questions of abortion and birth control; in sociology of religion you need the latest insights into the rapidly changing race issues; in psychology of religion you require the most recent studies of the relations between Christian mysticism and hallucinogenic drugs. For all these topics recent periodical articles are indispensable.

Periodical articles can also be invaluable as supplements to books. If you cannot find enough information in books, periodical articles may provide another source of information. Such a need may not depend on the latest periodicals but may be satisfied by articles more than fifty years old. For example, if books fail to give you enough discussion of the various interpretations of Matthew 10:34, you could benefit from a scholarly periodical article published in 1920 or earlier. An example is shown in FIGURE 28.

Using Indexes to Religious Periodicals

Locating such periodical articles is not a hopeless task, thanks to all the people who put together the periodical in-

dexes. Most religion majors have often used the *Readers' Guide to Periodical Literature*, which indexes popular and semipopular periodicals. However, few religion majors have even heard of *Religion Index One: Periodicals*, which indexes over 300 scholarly, religious periodicals. This index was begun in 1949, comes out semiannually, and has biennial cumulations. For a fuller description, see Chapter 5.

Like the card catalog, periodical indexes can be approached both through the relevant Bible texts and through regular subject headings. FIGURE 23, taken from *Religion Index One: Periodicals*, shows both approaches to recent articles on peace.

Note that the entries under "Bible. New Testament. Matthew Chapters 3-10" are arranged alphabetically by title, rather than by scriptural text. "Mt 10:34" in the illustration is Jesus' oft-quoted saying, "Do not think I have come to bring peace on earth; I have not come to bring peace, but a sword" (R.S.V.). "Expos T" should be looked up in the "Periodicals Indexed," inside the front cover of the index, where it is decoded as *Expository Times*. Many libraries put a mark here beside the titles they receive, in order to speed the readers' search. The rest of the entry, "81: 115-8 Ja '70," provides the volume number, pagination, and date.

The article highlighted in FIGURE 23 under "Revolution (Theology)" is of special interest because its title seems to imply an acceptance of revolution. If so, it is doubly surprising, because it was published in *Brethren Life*, a journal of one of the historic peace churches. However, such questions can be quickly answered in the affirmative without having to find the article itself. The asterisk at the end of the citation means that an abstract of the article appears in the "Author Index with Abstracts" section of the same volume of *Religion Index One: Periodicals*. Here it says that "This article shows that revolution is indigenous to the biblical message . . . " and "What is neded [sic] is a church backing the just revolution . . . . " Abstracts began appearing in *Religion Index One: Periodicals* in 1975.

Although a periodical index is far from the first place to look for a bibliography, this kind of source may, in fact, lead to a splendid bibliography. Perhaps the best bibliography on the minority view that Jesus was speaking of a literal sword is found in the article, "Uncomfortable Words. III. The Violent Word," which is cited in FIGURE 23. Several footnotes in this article cite works that deal with Jesus as a political revolutionary who advocated violence. Since this viewpoint is hard to find in the literature, but should nevertheless be recognized, these footnotes are an important discovery. Among those works cited is Samuel Brandon's *Jesus and*

BIBLE. NEW TESTAMENT. (Books and parts)
Matthew
  Theology (cont)
    La parabole du jugement dernier (Matthieu 25:31-46).
      J.C.Ingelaere. RHistPhRel 50 no 1:23-60 '70
    People and community in the gospel of Matthew.
      K.Tagawa. NTSt 16:149-62 Ja'70
    Die Polemik gegen Gesetzlosigkeit im ˉ
      Matthäus und bei Paulus: ʳ   ᵧ 652, St
      lichen Überlieferˉ   , ᴍatt 2:1-2] I.A.
      no 1:11ᵒ ˉˉ   ˉ ᵤe'69
    Cʰˉ   ˉˉ ᵤᵤten Unzialfragment des Matthäus-
            ˉᵤms [Lectionary 852, Matt 1:23-5, 2:1-27]
      ᴀ.Junack. NTSt 16:284-8 Ap'70

→ Chapters 3-10
    Ehescheidung nach alttestamentlichem und jüdischem Recht
      [Deut 24:1-4, Matt 5:32, 19:9, Mk 10:11] U.Nembach.
      ThZ 26:161-71 My-Je '70
    Focal instance as a form of New Testament speech; a study
      of Matthew 5:39b-42. R.C.Tannehill. JRel 50:372-85
      O'70
    Love your enemies; the historical setting of Matthew v:43f;
      Luke vi:27f. O.J.F.Seitz. NTSt 16:39-54 O'69
    Matthäus V:13a und 14a. G.Schwarz. NTSt 17:80-6 O'70
    Matthäus VI:9-13/Lukas XI:2-4; Emendation und
      Rückübersetzung. G.Schwarz. NTSt 15:233-47 Ja'69
    Matthäus 7:13a; ein Alarmruf angesichts höchster Gefahr.
      G.Schwarz. NovTest 12 no 2:229-32 '70
    Mission of the disciples and the mission charge; Matthew
      10 and parallels. F.W.Beare. JBibLit 89:1-13 Mr'70
    Mit welchem Mass ihr messt, wird euch gemessen werden
      [Mt 7:2, Gen 38:25-26] H.P.Rüger. ZNeutW 60 no 3-4:
      174-82 '69
    Realisierbare Forderungen der Bergpredigt? E.Lerle.
      KerDo 16 no 1:32-40 '70
    Uncomfortable words. I. The angry word: Matthew 5:21f.
      C.F.D.Moule. ExposT 81:10-13 O'69
→ Uncomfortable words. III. The violent word [Mt 10:34; cf
      Lk 12:51] M.Black. ExposT 81:115-8 Ja'70
    Uncomfortable words. VI. Fear him who can destroy
      both soul and body in hell [Mt 10:28] [Lk 12:4f] I.H.
      Marshall. ExposT 81:276-80 Je'70
    Das Wort von der Selbstbestattung der Toten; Beobachtun-
      gen zur Auslegungsgeschichte von Mt VIII:22 Par [Lk
      IX:59] H.G.Klemm. NTSt 16:60-75 O'69
    Zum Text der zweiten Vaterunserbitte [Mt 6, Lk 11]
      R.Freudenberger. NTSt 15:419-32 Jl'69
      see also

Subject Index

REVOLUTION (THEOLOGY)
Any alternative to complicity or conspiracy: aspects of the development of
the English-speaking churches in S Africa since World War II. Cook,
Calvin W. *J Th So Africa* No 27,4-19 Je 79*
Christliche und humane Sozialethik; übor von K Eifrig. Wingren, Gustaf.
Z Ev Ethik 24,288-302 O 80
Einige Aspekte sozialen Denkens im Ökumenischen Rat der Kirchen;
übers von B Williams [reply by R Alves, pp 215-216]. Lochman, Jan M.
Z Ev Ethik 23,206-215 Jl 79*
Royal idolatry: Peter Martyr and the Reformed tradition. Anderson, Mar-
vin W. *Archiv* 69,157-200 1978
The theologians and the peasants: conservative evangelical reactions to the
German Peasants Revolt. Kolb, Robert. *Archiv* 69,103-130 1978*
→ A theology of revolution. Doel, Anthonie van den. *Breth Life* 24,115-120
Spr 79*

Author Index with Abstracts

DOEL, Anthonie van den. A theology of revolution. *Breth Life* 24,115-120
Spr 79*.
→ This article shows that revolution is indigenous to the biblical message in
its eschatological aspects and ethical dimension. This is explained by reference to the confrontation with revolution in the developing world and in
Marxism, where its scope is limited. The church has supported the
→ counter-revolution, for the revolution could only be heard in prophetic,
messianic movements. What is needed is a church backing the just revolution, rather than a "just war", so that the goal of revolution, greater freedom, may be achieved.

FIGURE 23. American Theological Library Association. *Religion
Index One: Periodicals*, vol. 14 (1979-80), pp. 347, 519.

the Zealots, which is especially important because of its
moderately recent publication date, 1967, and the fact
that it was published by a university press, Manchester University Press. *Jesus and the Zealots* would presumably add
to the bibliography on the minority viewpoint.

Although Protestant periodicals predominate in *Religion
Index One: Periodicals*, this source is also useful to Roman
Catholics and Jews, because it includes a selection of Catholic and Jewish periodicals. In addition, the Protestant periodicals often discuss persons and topics important in Catholicism and Judaism.

Also broadly useful to students of all persuasions is the
major Catholic index, *The Catholic Periodical and Literature
Index, A Cumulative Author-Subject Index to a Selective
List of Catholic Periodicals and an Author-Title-Subject
Bibliography of Adult Books by Catholics with a Selection
of Catholic-Interest Books by Other Authors* (Haverford,
PA: Catholic Library Association, 1930--). Issued bimonthly
and cumulated biennially, this boon to scholars indexes 138
periodicals. *C.P.L.I.* indexes texts and commentaries of official documents of the Catholic Church, reviews of Catholic
books, and movie and play reviews. Since 1968, when the
book index, *Guide to Catholic Literature*, merged with
*Catholic Periodical Index, Catholic Periodical and Literature
Index* has also provided an author, title, and subject index
to books by Catholics or of interest to Catholics. Although
C.P.L.I. is especially strong in the field of religion, more than
half its entries deal with other disciplines. As FIGURE 24
shows, *C.P.L.I.* cites many articles under "Peace," including
one by the well-known activist, Father Daniel Berrigan.

PEACE
Abs, H. Grave peril of nuclear proliferation; interven-
  tion of Holy See delegate. OR (Eng) no.41 [498] 4
  O 13'77
Aubry, G., Bp. L'actualité sociale et politique a la
  Réunion; réflexions pastorales. Doc Cath 74:224-7
  Mr '77
Baum, W., Card. An Easter appeal for Peace. Origins
  6:701-2 Ap 21'77
Beifuss, J. Pax Christi mobilizes to escalate nonviolence.
  Nat Cath Rep 14:1+ N 18'77
Benelli, G., Abp. Brotherly love; homily at the Mass for
  Europe and for world peace. OR (Eng) no.6 [463] 4
  F 10'77
Benelli, G., Abp. Homélie ... en la Cathédrale de
  Strasbourg; pour l'Europe et la paix du monde. Doc
  Cath 74:152-4 F 20'77
→ Berrigan, D. What do you really believe about Church,
  peace and justice? ReligTJ 11:37-8 Mr'77
Bianchi, E. A national peace academy. America 139:
  405-6 D 2'78
    ˉ ᴅ. Northern Ireland 1977. OSVm 66:1 O 30'77.

    ˉˉᵗⁱᵒⁿ. Origins

FIGURE 24. *Catholic Periodical and Literature Index*, vol. 19
(1977-1978), p. 337.

Using Abstracts of Religious Articles

If you want to find articles on a particular scriptural passage, you will find that *New Testament Abstracts* (Cambridge, MA: Weston College School of Theology, 1956–) is quicker to use than *Religion Index One: Periodicals. New Testament Abstracts* has a fifteen-year (1956 to 1971) cumulative "Index of Principal Scripture Texts," as well as annual indexes after 1971. As shown in FIGURE 25, this indexes the verses in scriptural order. It only takes a second or two to see that an article on Luke 22:35-38 is abstracted, that is, condensed, in entry 905 (not page 905). On the other hand, *Religion Index One: Periodicals*, shown previously in FIGURE 23, groups several chapters together and arranges the articles by title, not in scriptural order. *New Testament Abstracts*, which is published three times a year and abstracts about 300 periodicals, also comes in handy if your library does not own a particular biblical periodical which you found cited in *Religion Index One: Periodicals* or in the *Catholic Periodical and Literature Index*. Or perhaps your library owns the periodical, but the article is in a language you cannot read. In either case, you can usually get a twenty-to-two-hundred-word abstract, which may tell you all you need to know. If you decide that you need the complete article, ask your reference librarian about getting a photocopy from another library.

As FIGURE 25 illustrates, entry 905 not only summarizes the article, but also cites the original source. Since the title of the article is in German, the article itself will also be in German. However, the abstract is in English, as you can see. It is interesting to note the author's idea that Luke justified both Christians who fled the war of A.D. 66-70 and those who fought in it. Most of the article is too specialized and scholarly for beginners, but an undergraduate might want to read the part of the article which states that the apostles' "reliance upon swords is their disobedience."

INDEX OF PRINCIPAL SCRIPTURE TEXTS

The numbers following the scriptural texts refer to entries, not pages.

Matthew	97r, 459—461, 839—847r	27:57—28:20	114	Luke	127—129, 500—501, 845, 886—892, 928r
1—2	98—99, 462, 848	28:2-4	480	1—2	98
1:1-17	849	28:18-20	481	1:1—9:50	502r
1:18-25	463—464, 850	28:19	862	1:1-4	893
1:25	851	28:19-20	115	1:2	894
3:1-12	465			1:26-38	463, 503, 850
		Mark	116—120, 412,	1:46-55	504, 895
				5	896
					130
					897
				17:20	465
				17:21	898
				17:26-30	9
				18:18-30	4>
				20:27-40	496
				21:5-36	137
				22:14-19	124
				22:14-38	904
				22:16-18	883
				22:35-38	905
				22:56-62	126
				23:29	513
				23:35-43	906
				24:12	138—139
				24:13-35	514

905. H.-W. Bartsch, "Jesu Schwertwort, Lukas xxii.35-38: Überlieferungsgeschichtliche Studie," *NTStud* 20 (2, '74) 190-203.

Redactional parallels (Lk 22:35 and 10:4), the formula of the citation of Isa 53:12 in v. 37 (*to gegrammenon*), the Lukan character of v. 37c and of the eschatological *dei* in v. 37a, and the omission of the solemn *amēn legō* (v. 37a), combined with the unlikelihood that the sword logion is a complete creation of either Luke or the church, suggest that vv. 35-38 are a Lukan reworking of a genuine Jesus-tradition. As such it had meaning for Luke's contemporary situation as well as for the exemplary time of Jesus. Its significance for Jesus' time is contained (1) in the citation of Isa 53:12, whereby Jesus is associated with two sword-bearing evildoers (23:32-33) and (2) in Jesus' response ("no, not yet," 22:51) to the disciples' assumption that the apocalyptic final battle is about to commence and that swords are therefore required. Luke, concerned for the unity of Judaism and Christianity after the war of A.D. 66-70 and mindful that in that war some Jewish Christians fled while others stayed, fought, and perished, now in his own day has a word for both. Verses 35-36 justify those who fled; those who fought, however, were also justified in that they too, like their Lord, were numbered among the transgressors. For Christians of the 20th century as of the 1st, this text denies to both sword-bearers and sword-deniers the right to stand in judgment of each other.—J.H.E.

906. W. Trilling, "Le Christ, roi crucifié. Lc 23, 35-43," *AssembSeign* 65 ('73) 56-65.

~~bout the account of the passion, Luke diverges a great deal from the
in this pericope. Luke avoids political titles as much as
the religious titles that express the
's account reveals the
as in Mk)

FIGURE 25. *New Testament Abstracts*, vol. 18 (1974), pp. 407, 311, 312.

As with periodical indexes, the periodical titles are abbreviated in the text and spelled out on a special page at the back of each issue.

Until 1978, students of the Old Testament had to struggle along without a reference source comparable to *New Testament Abstracts*. Now we have *Old Testament Abstracts* (Washington, DC: Catholic University of America, 1978--), which covers over 250 periodicals and has an "Index of Scripture Texts." At this writing *Old Testament Abstracts* has only six complete volumes, whereas *New Testament Abstracts* has twenty-six volumes, so there is much less chance of finding an article on a particular passage in *Old Testament Abstracts*.

One other possibility exists for finding abstracts of articles on the Old Testament before the genesis of *Old Testament Abstracts* in 1978. *Religious and Theological Abstracts* (Myerston, PA: Religious and Theological Abstracts, 1958--) is a quarterly that abstracts articles from 208 periodicals. However, its coverage of any given field of study is necessarily thin because its 208 periodicals cover not only biblical, but also theological, historical, and practical theology. Like *New Testament Abstracts* and *Old Testament Abstracts*, the primary use for this abstracting service is to give you a synopsis of an article which your library does not own or which is in a language you cannot read. *Religious and Theological Abstracts* has indexes to authors, subjects, and verses of scripture.

Using More Comprehensive Indexes

If the above sources fail or need to be supplemented, go to the most comprehensive continuing bibliography in biblical studies, *Elenchus Bibliographicus Biblicus* (Rome: Biblical Institute Press, 1920--). This monumental source is an annual multilingual bibliography of articles, books, book reviews, and dissertations. Now *Elenchus* is a separate publication, but before 1968 it was a part of the periodical *Biblica*. As FIGURE 26 shows, the index is in Latin, which means that you will look under "Lucas" for information on Luke. "X-4," which directly follows "Lucas," indicates that most references to Luke are in part 10, section 4 of the work. In the 1975 volume, published in 1978, section 4 was comprised of 178 items, about half arranged by author and half arranged by scriptural verse. The index, as shown in FIGURE 26, also cites works on individual verses of Luke. "Lucas 22, 35-37" refers to item 3240, where you find the wrong article, one dealing with Luke 22:66-23:49. However, the desired item is directly below it at item 3241, so the incorrect citation did not cause the item to be lost. In fact, item 3241 turns out to be a doctoral dissertation on the controversial passage in which Christ tells his disciples they may need to sell their cloaks in order to buy swords. The rather cryptic "Cf DissAbstr 35 (1974s) 1742s-A" means that you

can read a summary of the dissertation in *Dissertation Abstracts International*, volume 35, 1974, page 1742A. Many academic libraries have *Dissertation Abstracts International*, but they are unlikely to have the dissertation itself, which can be expected to have an extensive bibliography on the passage. Therefore you may want to ask your reference librarian to borrow or buy the dissertation for you. More on this in Chapter 9.

The best verse by verse index to the Gospels is *A Periodical and Monographic Index to the Literature on the Gospels and Acts* (Pittsburgh: Pittsburgh Theological Seminary, Clifford E. Barbour Library, 1971). This work, which is 336

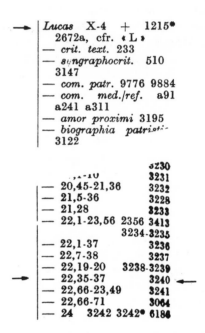

3239 — *Knudsen* J., The Problem of the Two Cups (Lk 22,19b-20): LuthQ 2 (1950) 74-85.

3240 2 2 , 6 6 - 2 3 , 4 9 : *Walaskay* P. W., Jr., The Trial and Death of Jesus in the Gospel of Luke : JBL 94 (1975) 81-93.

3241 2 2 , 3 5 - 3 7 : **Gormiley** J. F., The Final Passion Prediction : A Study of Lk 22 : 35-38. Diss. Fordham Univ. 1974 [Order No. 74-19.660]. 199 p. — Cf. DissAbstr 35 (1974s) 1742s-A.

3242 2 4 , 1 - 5 2 : **Guillaume** P., Tradition et Pastorale dans les récits lucaniens de la Résurrection et de l'Ascension. Diss. Strasbourg 1972/1973.

3242* *Kudasiewicz* J., Jeruzalem – miejscem ukazywań się zmartwychwstałego Chrystusa (Łk 24,1-52) ; Jérusalem – lieu des apparitions du Christ ressuscité (Lc 24,1-52) : RoTKan 21,1 (1974) 51-60.60.

3243 2 4 , 1 3 - 3 5 : *Bravo* C., El camino de Emaús : RJav 81 (1974) 396-403.

FIGURE 26. Biblical Institute Press. *Elenchus Bibliographicus Biblicus*, vol. 56 (1975), pp. 877, 879, 243.

pages long, cites books and articles published from 1952 to 1968. As FIGURE 27 illustrates, the index is in scriptural order, which means that reference to a 1959 article on Luke 22:35-51, entitled "Swords of Offence," can be found quickly.

Luke 22.33-34   645.15

Die Verleugnung des Petrus.
Von Eta Linnemann.
Z.Theol.& Kirche, 63. 1966. p.1-32.

→ Luke 22.35-51   607.1

→ Swords of Offence.
By S.G.Hall.
Studia Evangelica. p.499-502.
Texte & Untersuchungen. 73.
Berlin   Akademie-Verlag   1959

FIGURE 27. A Periodical and Monographic Index to the Literature on the Gospel and Acts

Using Indexes to General Periodicals

Elenchus and the Barbour Library's index, both discussed above, are unlikely to be available in a library not specializing in religion. On the other hand, many college libraries will have either *Religion Index One: Periodicals* or the *Catholic Periodical and Literature Index* (discussed on page 24). If yours does not, then you will find that your most useful periodical index is the *Humanities Index* (New York: Wilson, 1916--). Its coverage is 1907 to date. From 1965 to 1974 it was titled *Social Sciences & Humanities Index* and before 1965 its title was *International Index*. You may want to use the *Humanities Index*, even if your library owns the *Catholic Periodical and Literature Index* or *Religion Index One: Periodicals*, because the latter sources were begun in 1930 and 1949 respectively, and are no help for locating periodical articles before those dates. The *International Index* covered nine religious periodicals before *Religion Index One: Periodicals* became available.

As FIGURE 28 shows, the *International Index* cites an article which could be useful even though it was published more than fifty years ago, because its title sounds extremely relevant to our topic and it is lengthy. Before Metzger's cumulated *Index to Periodical Literature on Christ and the Gospels* (FIGURE 3) came out in 1966, a student would not have been likely to have found this article without searching in the *International Index*.

Currently the *Humanities Index* covers nineteen religion

periodicals, but only three of these, *American Jewish History, The Catholic Historical Review*, and *Studies in Comparative Religion* are not indexed in *Religion Index One: Periodicals*. You should use current volumes of *Humanities Index* as well as *Social Sciences Index* (1965 to date) because of their superb coverage of the leading scholarly journals in the humanities and social sciences, except for the disciplines of art and education. So many topics in religion are interdisciplinary that articles on religion frequently appear in the so-called secular journals of philosophy, history, literature, sociology, and the like. Also, the *Humanities Index* and the *Social Sciences Index* are easy to use, because they are identical to the *Readers' Guide* in format. Students whose libraries do not have *Religion Index One: Periodicals* or *Catholic Periodical and Literature Index* will find that the *Humanities Index* is their best available periodical index for religion.

Current articles on religious topics are also indexed in the *Readers' Guide to Periodical Literature*, 1900-- (New York: Wilson, 1905--). The following predecessors give coverage back to 1802: *Poole's Index to Periodical Literature*, 1802-1906 (vol. 1, Boston: Osgood, 1882; vols. 2-6, Boston: Houghton, 1888-1908); and *Nineteenth Century Readers' Guide to Periodical Literature*, a two-volume work which covers 1890 to 1899 with supplementary indexing for 1900 to 1922 (New York: Wilson, 1944). The great problem in using the *Readers' Guide* is selecting articles by reputable scholars, who often write for such periodicals as *Atlantic, Harper's*, and *The New York Times Magazine*. Unless you recognize an author, it is advisable to avoid articles in such popular periodicals as *Reader's Digest* and *Good Housekeeping*.

616

Jesus Christ —Continued
Teaching
Changeless gospel and the modern mind. W. T. Davison. Lond Q R 109:1-20 Ja '08
Christ and the law of contradiction. F. W. O. Ward. Lond Q R 119:289-301 Ap '13
Christ's estimate of the human personality. L. Reddin. Bib Sac 71:132-44 Ja '14
→ Christ's sanction as well as condemnation of war. J. M. Wilson. Hibbert J 13:839-58 Jl '15
Christ's teaching about marriage. G: B. Eager. Constr Q 1:611-18 S '13
Ethical teaching of Jesus. J: S. Banks. Lond Q R 120:145-7 Jl '13
Gospel of Krishna and of Christ. M. Joynt. Hibbert J 6:77-89 O '07
Hope of the world. Spec 102:568-9 Ap 10 '09
Judge and a divider. Spec 99:701-2 N 9 '07
Lacunae in the gospels. Spec 103:635-6 O 23 '09
Religious teaching of Jesus, by C. G. Montefiore. Review. Spec 104:1064-6 Je 25 '10
Reservations of Jesus. Spec 102:733-4 My 8 '09
Significance of Jesus for modern relig⸍ view of his eschatological te⸍⸍ Scott. Am J Theol 18:22⁵ ⸍⸍
Teaching of Jesus—⸍ Brash. Lond ⸍
Tolstov'⸍

FIGURE 28. International Index

27

For current topics in religion, as well as for topics of continuing interest, the use of the *Readers' Guide* can be recommended simply because it indexes *America* and *Commonweal*, two important Roman Catholic periodicals not indexed in *Religion Index One: Periodicals*.

Using A Computer to Search *Religion Index One* and *Two*

You may want to consider asking your librarian to do a computer search if you are faced with a time-consuming search in periodical indexes. A student can easily spend more than an hour examining several subject headings in many volumes. In this case, a computer search is not only faster; it is more thorough.

How is this possible? It is possible because all the significant words (omitting articles, prepositions, and conjunctions) for each article listed in a periodical index have been "loaded" into a computer. This enables the computer to find articles for you not only by subject headings, but also by words in titles and abstracts. Of course it would be impractical for a student to open up each volume of *Religion Index One: Periodicals* and read through all the titles and abstracts looking for certain key words, but a librarian using a computer can do this in a few seconds.

Religion Index One: Periodicals and *Religion Index Two: Multi-Author Works* can be searched at the same time by using a library computer terminal that is connected by phone to a powerful computer in New York. For example, if you are looking for articles on Christ's teaching about the sword, you might start by searching for citations containing both the words "Christ" and "sword." These two words, of course, suggest related words that can be searched. FIGURE 29 shows a computer search covering 1949 through January 1984 for articles in which the words "sword" or "swords" appear in the same citation as words beginning with "Jesus" or "Christ." The dollar sign after "Christ," near the top of FIGURE 29 is a symbol which tells the computer that you want to find articles not only with the word "Christ" but those with "Christ's," "Christian," "Christian's," "Christianity," and any other word that might begin with "Christ." As shown at the top of FIGURE 29, 73 citations contain the words "sword" or "swords" and 11,777 citations contain words beginning with "Jesus" or "Christ." Of course, a student doing research on Christ's teaching on the sword would want to know which of the 73 sword citations also mention Jesus or Christ. As shown in statement number 3, FIGURE 29, the answer ("result") is 7. Statement 4 shows a request to print ("..p") the titles ("ti") of the most recent six documents from statement 3. The most relevant of the six appear to be documents 3, 4, and 6, so next is requested all the information available ("all") for these three documents. Note that the title (and therefore the text) of document 4 is in German, but the abstract ("AB") is in English. Note also that the title of document 6 has none of the key words being searched, but the computer found them in the abstract. At

```
BRS/RELI/1949 - JAN 1984

BRS - SEARCH MODE  - ENTER QUERY
    1_:   sword or swords
    RESULT

    2_:   Jesus$ or Christ$
E1417 MORE THAN 100 TERMS FOR CHRIST$
LAST TERM PROCESSED WAS CHRISTENSENC-C A

    RESULT    11777

    3_:   1 and 2
    RESULT         7

    4_:   ..p 3 ti/doc=1-6
     1
TI THOMAS MUNTZER AND THE SWORD OF GIDEON.

     2
TI 'HANDING OVER TO SATAN': AN EXPLANATION OF 1 COR 5:1-7.

     3
TI THE SWORD-WORD OF JESUS, LK 22:35-38.

     4
TI CHRISTENTUM ALS ALTERNATIVE ZUM MARXISMUS.

     5
TI THE SWORD OF THE SPIRIT: THE MEANING OF INSPIRATION.

     6
TI BETWEEN WAR AND PEACE: OLD DEBATE IN A NEW AGE.
           END OF DOCUMENTS

_:    ..p 3 all/doc= 3,4,6
     3
AN 300104.  (RI).  8308.
AU BARTSCH-HANS-W.
TI THE SWORD-WORD OF JESUS, LK 22:35-38.
SO BRETH LIFE.  19 NO 3,149-155 SUM 74.
YR 74.
LG EN.
DE BIBLE-NT: LUKE: CHAPTERS-20-24.  ZEALOTS-JEWISH-PARTY.  PACIFISM.
   LIBERATION-THEOLOGY.
     4
AN 003347.  (RI).  0000.
AU KUHN-HELMUT.
TI CHRISTENTUM ALS ALTERNATIVE ZUM MARXISMUS.
SO INT KATH Z.  4,257-265.  MY-JE 75.
YR 75.
LG GE.
DE COMMUNISM-AND-CHRISTIANITY.
AB A GROUP OF MODERN THEOLOGIANS ARE EAGER TO BRING CHRISTIANITY UP TO
   DATE BY ADOPTING MARXIST IDEAS.  AT THE SAME TIME THEY JOIN HANDS
   WITH MARXISTS IN SYMPATHY WITH A FAITH THAT MERCIFULLY EMBRACES THE
   CAUSE OF THE DISINHERITED OF THE EARTH.  HOWEVER, NO AFFINITIES OF
   SENTIMENT AND ATTITUDE ENTITLE THESE MEDIATORS TO IGNORE OR BELITTLE
   THE EITHER/OR WHICH SEPARATES THE SERMON ON THE MOUNT FROM THE
   COMMUNIST MANIFESTO.  MARXIST FAITH IS INSPIRED BY A MILITANT
   CHILIASM THAT INVOKES A SAVIOUR WITH THE SWORD, WHEREAS THE KINGDOM
   OF GOD AS PREACHED BY CHRIST IS NOT OF THIS WORLD.  HENCE THE
   CHRISTIAN TURNING MARXIST CEASES TO BE A CHRISTIAN AND VICE VERSA.

     6
AN 223192.  (RI).  0000.
AU CULVER-ROBERT-D.
TI BETWEEN WAR AND PEACE: OLD DEBATE IN A NEW AGE.
SO CHR T.  24,30-34 O 24 1980.
YR 80.
LG EN.
DE CHURCH-AND-STATE: HISTORY-OF-DOCTRINES.  WAR-AND-RELIGION.  PACIFISM.
AB THE IDEA OF NON-RESISTANCE TO EVIL IN JESUS' TEACHING WAS OBSERVED IN
   THE FIRST THREE CENTURIES BY CHRISTIANS, FOR THESE REASONS: 1) JESUS'
   EXAMPLE, 2) IDOLATRY IN ARMY LIFE, 3) A GOVERNMENT THAT THREW
   CHRISTIANS TO THE LIONS, 4) VINDICATION IN THE WORLD TO COME, 5)
   CHRISTIANS DOING MORE GOOD BY NON-MILITARY ACTIVITY, AND 6)
   EXPECTATION OF CHRIST'S RETURN TO DESTROY THE EMPIRE.  BUT AFTER
   CONSTANTINE, CHRISTIANS ADJUSTEDTO CHRISTIAN PARTICIPATION IN
   MILITARY DEFENCE OF A 'CHRISTIAN' GOVERNMENT.  THEY ALSO CAME TO SEE
   THAT GOVERNMENT OF SINFUL MEN BY COERCIVE POWER IS BIBLICALLY-ROOTED
   IN NECESSITY OCCASIONED BY THE FALL OF MAN.  THE ROMAN CHURCH TENDED
   TO ROOT THE POWER OF GOVERNMENT IN THE ORDER OF CREATION; THE
   REFORMERS IN THE DOCTRINE OF SIN AND OF PROVIDENCE.  THE ANABAPTIST
   MOVEMENT DEVELOPED TOWARD A NON-RESISTANCE (PACIFISM) NOT UNLIKE THAT
   OF THE EARLY CHURCH.  MENNONITES AND DUNKERS (BRETHREN) BELIEVE THE
   EXAMPLE AND TEACHING OF JESUS FORBID CHRISTIANS FROM BEARING ARMS OR
   PERSONAL DEFENSE.  THEY DO NOT, HOWEVER, THINK GOVERNMENT MUST GIVE
   UP ITS 'POWER OF THE SWORD'--ONLY THAT CHRISTIANS AS CITIZENS OF THE
   KINGDOM OF GOD MAY NOT PARTICIPATE.  (EXCERPT).

           END OF DOCUMENTS

_:    ..off
*CONNECT TIME   0:06:12 HH:MM:SS    0.103 DEC HRS    SESSION   301*

EST RELI COST:   C-HRS    DB-ROY  CIT-ROY   COMM    TOTAL

                 $1.65    $1.55    $.08     $.82    $4.10

*SIGN-OFF  13.48.34                02/07/84:
```

FIGURE 29. Computer search of Religion Index. Printed by permission of BRS.

the bottom of FIGURE 29 you can read that this search took 6 minutes and 12 seconds at a total cost of $4.10. Computer searches often cost $10 to $20 or more. Some libraries provide this service free as part of their reference service, but most require students to pay part or all of the cost.

The ability to search *Religion Index One* and *Religion Index Two* is now available only by contract with BRS, a company which sells such searches in many other indexes as well. Several hundred indexes in many disciplines are available for computerized searching in many academic libraries who have contracts not only with BRS but with similar services. For some topics in religion you may want to consider computerized searching in psychology, sociology, or history. Your reference librarian can tell you what is available.

As this chapter has demonstrated, periodical articles are crucial to the study of currently debated topics, and they can be located through a variety of indexes. A student who makes use of these indexes will unearth treasures that other students will never find.

Summary

1. The primary reason for using periodical indexes is to locate articles on topics of current controversy, but they are also useful to locate articles that supplement the book collection.

2. Two of the most important indexes to religious periodicals are *Religion Index One: Periodicals* and the *Catholic Periodical and Literature Index*.

3. Two periodicals which give condensations of biblical articles are *New Testament Abstracts* and *Old Testament Abstracts. Religious and Theological Abstracts* provides somewhat thin coverage of the four major areas of theological studies.

4. Two of the most comprehensive indexes to articles on the Bible are *Elenchus Bibliographicus Biblicus* and *A Periodical and Monographic Index to the Literature on the Gospels and Acts*.

5. The *Readers' Guide* and the *Humanities Index* cover a broad range of periodicals and are widely available. They cite many articles of interest to students of religion.

6. A computer can provide fast, in-depth searching of *Religion Index One: Periodicals* and *Religion Index Two: Multi-Author Works*.

A word fitly spoken is like apples of gold in pictures of silver. Prov. 25:11

Quotations to Improve Sermons and Term Papers

Knowing how to find quotations is probably more important to seminarians than to other students of religion, because apt quotations are so vital to preaching. A quotation can be the most memorable part of a sermon.

But any student can strengthen a term paper by means of well-chosen quotations. They constitute an appeal to authority supported by the authority's own words. If you are arguing that Jesus was a pacifist, you might want to quote a 1932 report of the Federal Council of Churches of Christ in America: "To support war is to deny the gospel

---

WAR, JUST

The only constraint to wage war is defense against an injustice of the utmost gravity which strikes the entire community and which cannot be coped with by any other means.
　　POPE PIUS XII, *Address*, October 19, 1953

The occasions to which the concept of the just war can be rightly applied have become highly restricted. A war to "defend the victims of wanton aggression" where the demands of justice join the demands of order, is today the clearer case of a just war. . . . The concept of a just war does not provide moral justification for initiating a war of incalculable consequences to end such oppression.
　　ANGUS DUN and REINHOLD NIEBUHR, *Christianity and Crisis*, June 13, 1955

The Kingdom of God cannot take the responsibility for defending itself in arms: that is the lesson of the New Testament. But the New Testament nowhere forbids the secular powers to defend the Kingdom of God, when unjustly attacked.
　　CHARLES JOURNET, *The Church of the Word Incarnate*, Vol. I, 1955

→ There may come into existence in a nation a situation in which all hope of averting

war becomes vain. In this situation a war of efficacious self-defense against unjust attacks, which is undertaken with hope of success, cannot be considered illicit.
　　POPE PIUS XII, *Christmas Message*, 1956

The morality of the violence will depend on its proportion to the aggression. One will not rout a burglar with an atomic bomb.
　　JOHN R. CONNEY, *Theology Digest*, Winter, 1957

Always look out, my young friend, when the theologians start talking about a just war. It is such a comprehensive and reasonable phrase that it really ought to be prohibited.
　　HEINRICH BÖLL, *Letter to a Young Catholic*, 1958

To be finally justified there should be some reasonable expectation that a war can produce more good than evil, or at least achieve a lesser evil than not resorting to arms would lead to.
　　PAUL RAMSEY, *War and the Christian Conscience*, 1961

See also Aggression; Injustice; Peace; Rights; Self-Defense; War; War, Defense of.

FIGURE 30. The World Treasury of Religious Quotations

which we profess to believe." On the other hand, if you want to defend the just war as a Christian concept, you could quote a 1956 Christmas message by Pope Pius XII: "There may come into existence in a nation a situation in which all hope of averting war becomes vain. In this situation a war of efficacious self-defense against unjust attacks, which is undertaken with hope of success, cannot be considered illicit."

How can you find such apt quotations? The easy way is to use a book of quotations that is arranged topically. Ralph L. Woods, *The World Treasury of Religious Quotations* (New York: Hawthorn, 1966), as shown in FIGURE 30, is a quotation book especially useful for religion students because its quotes are selected for their religious message. Woods has ten pages on the subject of war, with subheadings including "War, Unjust" and "War, Just." It happens that both the quotations in the previous paragraph appear in these ten pages of Woods' book.

The best of the secular quotation books is Burton Stevenson, *Home Book of Quotations*, 10th ed. (New York:

Dodd, Mead, 1967), which happens to have fifteen pages of quotations on war, and they are subdivided into twelve sections under such headings as "War: Its Virtues" and "War: Its Horrors."

Three Uses of Quotation Books

One use for quotation books is to verify a partially remembered quotation. If you can remember a key word or phrase, you may be able to find the full quotation and its author by using the key word index in a quotation book. As illustrated in FIGURE 31, if you want the full quotation for "there never was a good war," read through the index to *The Home Book of Quotations* under "war," until you come to "never was good w. 2118: 8." This tells you to look on page 2118, item 8, where you read, "There never was a good war or a bad peace," written by Benjamin Franklin in a *Letter to Quincy* (11 September 1773).

You can also use such a collection of quotations on a

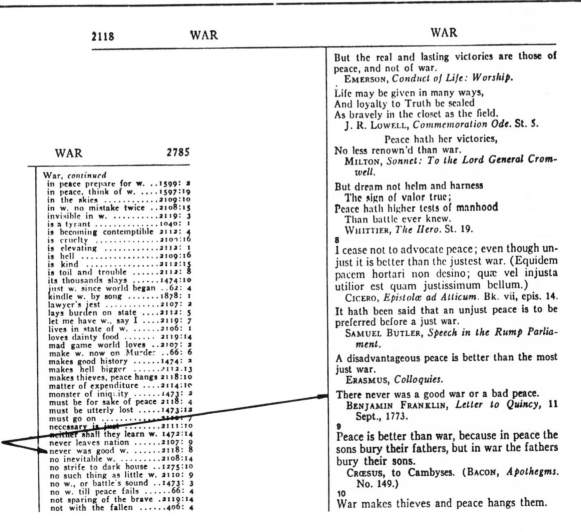

FIGURE 31. The Home Book of Quotations

single topic to stimulate your thinking, to introduce you to new ideas. For example, when reading through the ten pages on war in Woods' book, you would come across William James' call "to discover something heroic in the social realm that is the moral equivalent of war." This might lead you to consider the Great Commission (Matthew 28:18-20) and the heroic lives of the saints.

Another side benefit of quotation books is that they can strengthen your bibliography. For example, in reading the section on war in *The World Treasury of Religious Quotations*, you come across Martin Luther's statement, "War is the greatest plague that can afflict humanity; it destroys religion, it destroys states, it destroys families. Any scourge is preferable to it." You note that it is a quotation from *Table Talk*. This makes you eager to look in his *Table Talk* and his other works to see what else the great reformer had to say about war. Of course, this would be a question more appropriate to a church history course than to a Bible course.

Perhaps a concluding word of caution is in order. Do not allow yourself to become hypnotized by the quantity of gemlike quotations. A term paper should be primarily your own creation, not a mosaic of others' words or ideas.

Summary

1. Future preachers, as well as other students of religion, can strengthen their writing by means of apt quotations.
2. Quotations are found most easily in books of quotations arranged by topic.
3. Quotation books stimulate your thinking, strengthen your bibliography, and enable you to verify a half-remembered quote.
4. Do not use too many quotations.

8 Using Guides to the Literature of Religion

How can I, except some man should guide me?
Acts 8:31

Why Use a Guide

This book is a *selective* guide to the *basic* reference sources in religion, and therefore it may not be telling everything you need to know. Especially if you are an advanced student, you may need a more comprehensive guide in order to find specialized reference sources which bear closely on your topic. Guides to the literature of a subject and comprehensive lists of reference sources can lead to materials in your library and also point out the existence of materials not in your library collection. Reference librarians rely heavily on these guides and lists, and if finding enough material is a problem, you should be aware of such guides too. The main problem with comprehensive guides is to select the few sources that are needed from the many that are cited.

How to Use Guides to Religious Reference Sources

The most useful comprehensive guide to reference sources in religion is Robert J. Kepple, *Reference Works for Theological Research; An Annotated, Selective Bibliographical Guide*, 2nd ed., (Washington, DC: University Press of America, 1981). It briefly describes about eight hundred encyclopedias, handbooks, bibliographies, and other kinds

---

Biblical Studies: Biblio. Guides

**GENERAL--NEW TESTAMENT

AA21. Scholer, David M. A Basic Bibliographic Guide for New Testament Exegesis. 2nd ed. Grand Rapids: Eerdmans, 1973.
This and France (immediately below) complement one another. Scholer provides better coverage of the central topics of N.T. study. Entries are topically arranged, and include some annotation and discussion. The final section lists 3 to 5 "best" commentaries on each N.T. book. Author index.

AA22. France, R. T. A Bibliographical Guide to New Testament Research. 3rd ed. Sheffield, England: J.S.O.T. Press, 1979.
Like Scholer, also includes listings for O.T., inter-testamental, early church, and other background tools. Concentrates more on background information and reference works -- no commentary listings. Some annotations & discussion, British orientation. Includes a list of 49 periodicals of particular importance in N.T. research.

AA23. Gaffron, H.-G., and Stegemann, H. Systematisches Verzeichnis der wichtigsten Fachliteratur für das Theologiestudium: Vorausdruck für das Einzelfach Neues Testament, gemäss dem Stand im Frühjahr 1966. Bonn: H. Bouvier, 1966.
A selective bibliography for the study of the New Testament which was written to be part of a larger work (never published). Classified arrangement, no annotations, name index. Special characteristics of the books (e.g. "priority for acquisition") are indicated through symbols (see p. 12).

FIGURE 32. Robert J. Kepple, *Reference Works for Theological Research: An Annotated Selective Bibliographical Guide*, p. 115. Published in 1981 by University Press of America. Reprinted by permission.

of reference sources under such chapter titles as "Christian Ethics" and "Ancient Church History & Patristics." To point up its usefulness for a Bible student, there is a chapter entitled "Biblical Studies; Bibliographical Guides" which annotates fifteen guides, including several which evaluate commentaries. Notice in FIGURE 32 that Scholer "lists 3 to 5 'best' commentaries on each N. T. book." Kepple often reports that a work is written from an evangelical point of view. However, he includes few works by or about the Roman Catholic church because that area of study is so well covered by James Patrick McCabe, O.S.F.S., *Critical Guide to Catholic Reference Books*, 2nd ed., (Littleton, CO: Libraries Unlimited, 1980). McCabe's guide describes over 1,100 titles relating to Catholicism, including those dealing with the social sciences, the arts, and literature — "subjects to which Catholics have traditionally contributed a unique perspective."

Comparable to Kepple but not quite as complete or as current is John A. Bollier, *The Literature of Theology; A Guide for Students and Pastors* (Philadelphia: Westminster, 1979). Bollier's book grew out of his course in theological research at Yale Divinity School.

One other guide deserves mention because it annotates books from an evangelical perspective. Cyril J. Barber, *The Minister's Library*, 2 vols. (Grand Rapids, MI: Baker Book House, 1974-1983), briefly describes and evaluates books, not just reference books, in eleven broad categories, such as New Testament, pastoral theology, and comparative religions.

How to Use a Guide to General Reference Sources

The most comprehensive annotated bibliography of reference sources in English is: A.J. Walford, *Walford's Guide to Reference Material*, 4th ed., 3 vols. (London: The Library Association, 1980--). Volume 2, 1982, has a thirty-nine page section on religion which is comparable in scope to Kepple, except that Walford has ten pages on non-Christian religions, whereas Kepple omits this subject.

This chapter has commented on a few of the most useful guides to religion in general and shown how to find guides useful to Bible students. Guides for other religion courses, such as church history, are also cited in Appendix 2, along with other general guides that are fairly recent and comprehensive.

Summary

1. Guides to the literature of religion may help you locate specialized materials useful for your paper.
2. Bible students can get this help from guides to the literature of the Bible.
3. Guides to the literature of other religion courses appear in Appendix 2.

It is satisfying to use bibliographies, periodical indexes, and abstracts, when they lead you to vital books and articles in your library. However, these reference sources can also be frustrating if, after locating some choice items, you find that your library does not own them. This happens to students and faculty even at the largest theological libraries. Fortunately, the problem is not insoluble if you act in time.

How to Request Materials from Other Libraries

Your reference librarian may be able to borrow the books you need from another library, and he may be able to get you photocopies of any articles you need. All he needs is time, a full and accurate citation, and, in the case of photocopying, some cash. The time required varies from a few days to a few months, depending on whether your library is part of a cooperating network of libraries and whether the material is available in the library where it is requested. An average wait is about two weeks. The full citation generally required includes a report of the page where you found the book or article cited. This may seem like bureaucratic red tape, but this information is required by lending libraries and is good insurance against errors in transmission. If you do not have the full bibliographical information, ask your reference librarian to help you find it. The cost of photocopies is usually ten cents or more per exposure. Libraries often make no charge for mailing books, but they seldom mail the periodicals themselves.

If you are an undergraduate at a university, you may find that this interlibrary loan service is not available to you, primarily because a university library serving doctoral students is presumed to have a collection that is adequate for undergraduates. Interlibrary loan service is more readily available to undergraduates at colleges, which often have made special arrangements to borrow from a nearby university or a state library.

Visiting Another Library

If a seminary or large university library is close, your time is short, or your library will not borrow for you, then you may prefer to visit another library. Your reference librarian can give you the address, phone number, subject specialties, and perhaps the hours of most libraries you may want to visit. You might ask him which theological seminaries are closest and whether you will need a pass or letter of introduction in order to use the library. Most libraries let visitors use materials in the library only.

If you need a particular periodical, your reference librarian can help you find which nearby libraries own it. He finds the locations of periodicals by using the *Union List of Serials, New Serial Titles* and other sources. With a little help, you can do the same.

Books are harder to locate, but the *National Union Catalog*, published 1953 to date, and the *National Union Catalog, Pre-1956 Imprints*, published 1968-1980, do give the locations of a good many books. Most academic libraries also can locate books by using a computer terminal. For example, OCLC is a computer service that provides information as to which of more than 4,300 libraries have any books you might want.

Using the *Library of Congress Catalog – Books: Subjects*

If you are having difficulty finding enough books on your topic, consult the subject-arranged book catalog of the world's largest library: Library of Congress, *Library of Congress Catalog – Books: Subjects; A Cumulative List of Works Represented by Library of Congress Printed Cards*, (Washington: Library of Congress, 1955--). Its five-year cumulations and quarterly supplements are a comprehensive subject listing of books published in the U.S. from 1950 to date. As FIGURE 33 shows, if you look in the 1970-1974 volumes under the heading "War and religion," you see that this source includes many foreign language publications, such as Toulat's book, and many pamphlets, such as Tolstoy's 11-page letter. Note the "see also" references under "War and religion," which provide a handy cumulation of subject headings comparable to the subject heading books which were discussed in Chapter 3. The supplements to this book update the record of subject headings but are cumbersome to use. Many college libraries do not own the *Library of Congress Catalog – Books: Subjects*, which in 1983 totalled 209 cumulative volumes covering from 1950 to 1974, but you may be able to visit a library which does have it. Whatever promising books you find there can be pursued through your own library and elsewhere.

When you visit another library, be sure to check its card catalog under the subject headings you found useful in your own library. The larger the religion collection, the more you can expect to find, and you may find some useful titles you have not seen in any bibliography.

Summary

1. Bibliographies and periodical indexes can be frustrating to use if your library does not own the materials cited.
2. You can ask your reference librarian to borrow books from other libraries or get photocopies of articles. Allow enough time for this procedure.
3. You can also visit other libraries, with help from your reference librarian.
4. The *Library of Congress Catalog – Books: Subjects* is a comprehensive subject bibliography that can lead you to books in other libraries.

⟶ WAR AND RELIGION

⟶ see also Conscientious objectors; Nonviolence; Pacifism; War and morals; World War, 1939-1945—Catholic Church; subdivision Religious aspects under specific wars, e.g. World War, 1939-1945—Religious aspects

Applewhite, Harry.
Waging peace: a way out of war. Philadelphia, Published for Joint Educational Development ₍by₎ United Church Press ₍1974₎
190 p. 22 cm. (A Shalom resource)
Includes bibliographies.
1. Peace. 2. War and religion. I. Joint Educational Development. II. Title.
JX1953.A6463   261.87′3   73-20080
ISBN 0-8298-0266-5   MARC

Austad, Torleiv.
Krig eller fred? Kristne synspunkter på krig/fred-problemet. Stavanger, Nomi, 1970.
148, ₍1₎ p. 18 cm. (Signal-bøkene) 14.00   N 70-25
BT736.2.A9   76-515407

Ballou, Adin, 1803-1890.
Christian non-resistance in all its important bearings. Appendix by William S. Heywood. New York, Da Capo Press, 1970.
xv, 278 p. ports. 23 cm. (Civil liberties in American history)
BT736.6.B34 1970   233   70-121104
SBN 306-71960-0   MARC

₍1803-1890.
…istance in all its important bearings, il-…ether with A discourse on …cases, and Christian … Ward Beecher,
Sweden. Utbildningsdeparte…   …iew of
Promemoria angående den fö… kyrkoberedskapsutredningens betänkand… akap (SOU 1965:59) Stockholm, 19
v. 30 cm. (Utbildningsdepartementet. ₍Publikatio…

CONTENTS:
del 2. Sammandrag av utredningens förslag och remissyttrandena.
1. Sweden—Religion. 2. War and religion. I. Sweden. Kyrko-beredskapsutredningen. Kyrklig beredskap. II. Title. III. Series: Sweden. Utbildningsdepartementet. Publikation 1970:7.
L501.A44 1970:7, etc.   73-345806

⟶ Tolstoi, Lev L'vovich, graf, 1869-1945.
Letter to a sergeant, by Leo Tolstoy; in reply to a letter of 18th December 1898 from Sergeant Michael Shalaginov (retired) asking whether Christian teaching is compatible with military service and war, ₍translated from the Russian₎. Bristol, M. S. Robinson & R. V. Sampson, 1969.
11 p. 22 cm. unpreed   B 69-10897
BT736.2.T6   261.873   74-463533
SBN 9500850-0-4   MARC

⟶ Toulat, Pierre.
Des évêques face au problème des armes. Dossier présenté par Pierre Toulat. ₍Paris₎ Éditions du Centurion ₍1973₎
167 p. 22 cm. 20.00F   F***
Includes bibliographical references.
1. War and religion. 2. Nonviolence—Moral and religious aspects. I. Title.
BT736.2.T68   261.873   74-157100
ISBN 2-227-31505-9   MARC

FIGURE 33. Library of Congress. Library of Congress Catalog. *Library of Congress Catalog – Books: Subjects; A Cumulative List of Works Represented by Library of Congress Printed Cards, 1970-1974.* Totowa, N.J.: Rowman and Littlefield, 1976, vol. 97, pp. 508, 509.

Therefore whosoever heareth these sayings of mine, and doeth them, I will liken him unto a wise man . . . . Matt. 7:24

Once I was standing with some other faculty members and was introduced to Krister Stendahl, of the Harvard Divinity School, with the words, "This is Jim Kennedy, from the library."

"Aren't we all?" he asked.

Perhaps you are not yet "from the library" and have been reading this guide without applying it to your own term paper. If so, let's hope Yogi Berra had the right idea, if not the right words, when he said, "You can observe a lot just by watching." Is it now time to learn by doing?

On the other hand, if you have been opening the reference books and carrying out your own library search as you read along, then you already have some of your reward, and in the life to come, i.e., after graduation, you will have one of the necessary skills for continuing your education.

John Hart, "B.C." comic strips. New York: Field Enterprises, 1971. By permission of John Hart and Field Enterprises, Inc.

TO CHOOSE YOUR TOPIC, BEGIN BROADLY by casting your
net over a wide area. Survey possible topics in encyclopedias,
textbooks, and reserve books.
　　NARROW the possible topics on the basis of your interests
　　and what is available in the library. Look for subdivisions
　　of the broad topics in encyclopedias, textbooks, and
　　reserve books.
　　　　NARROW further by using subject subdivisions
　　　　in the card catalog.
　　　　　Use chapters of books that you found under
　　　　　the most relevant subject headings.
　　　　　Use Bible concordances.

THE   CHOSEN   TOPIC

　　　　BEGIN to look for information
　　　　on your topic by using the subject
　　　　heading books and tracings to find the
　　　　most relevant subject headings in the card
　　　　catalog.
　　　　Browse among the most promising books found
　　　　in the card catalog by using the indexes of the
　　　　books, their bibliographies, and their footnotes. Also
　　　　use *Essay&General Literature Index* to find parts of books.
　　　　Use selective bibliographies as well as indexes to book re-
　　　　reviews and critiques, in order to evaluate books on which you
　　　　plan to base your paper. Also use biographical sources to evalu-
　　　　ate an author's creditials.
　　ENLARGE and update your available resources by using periodical
　　indexes and abstracts.
　　BROADEN your knowledge by using guides to the literature.
　　END by surveying the realms of recorded knowledge through the exploration
of comprehensive bibliographies that are arranged by subject. Consider getting
materials from other libraries. Strengthen your writing by using quotation books.

Appendix 1
Library Knowledge Test

A. Directions: Use this catalog card to answer the questions below.

```
                    The way to peace

BS
680        Topel, L. John.
.F7            The way to peace : liberation through
T66        the Bible / L. John Topel. --
           Maryknoll, N.Y. : Orbis Books, c1979.
              viii, 199 p. ; 24 cm.
              Includes bibliographical references
           and index.




              1. Freedom (Theology)--Biblical
           teaching.  2. Liberation theology.
           I. Title

           24 JAN 80     3892402   IEClat        78-9148
```

1. Would this card be filed with other cards beginning "B," "T," or "W"?
2. What is the subtitle?
3. Does the book mention other publications?
4. Under what other headings will cards for this book be found in the card catalog?

       *   *   *

B. Directions: Use this excerpt from the *Readers' Guide to Periodical Literature* to answer the following questions:

```
LIBERATION Front of Quebec. See Front for
   the Liberation of Quebec
LIBERATION theology
   Courteous condemnation. Chr Today 23:13 O 19
      '79
   Did the Pope apply the brakes at Puebla? D.
      Peerman. Chr Cent 96:203-4 F 28 '79
   Feminist theology in a global perspective. S.
      H. Lindley. il Chr Cent 96:465-9 Ap 25 '79
   Half a blessing: Pope John Paul II's CELAM
      message. Commonweal 106:68-9 F 16 '79
   John Paul vs liberation theology. il pors Time
      113:68-9 F 12 '79
   Liberation and El Salvador's Archbishop: O. A.
      Romero. P. Lacefield. Chr Cent 96:951-2 O 3
      '79
   Liberation theology and the Pope. M. Novak.
      Commentary 67:60-4 Je '79
   Liberation theology in a northern context. J.
      Langan. America 140:46-9 Ja 27 '79
   Pope and theologies of liberation. America 140:
      84 F 10 '79
   Putting on the tiara; contrast between John
      Paul II's and Cross currents' views on libera-
      tion theology. D. Vree. Nat R 31:424 Mr 30 '79
   Where has liberation theology gone wrong? W.
      D. Roberts. por Chr Today 23:26-8 O 19 '79
```

5. How do you find out the full title of the periodical that carries the article, "Putting on the Tiara"?
6. On what pages does "Pope and Theologies of Liberation" appear?
7. In what volume does it appear?
8. Who is its author?
9. Under what heading will you find articles on the Liberation Front of Quebec?
10. Does the article, "Feminist Theology in a Global Perspective," have any pictures?

The answers are at the bottom of the next page.

**Basic Reference Sources for Courses in
Religion and Theology**

Note: The first library search with any of the following course-related bibliographies will be easier if used in conjunction with Appendix 3, "Guidelines for Proceeding." To make it easier to locate materials, most items are cited as they appear on Library of Congress catalog cards.

Symbols: *   indicates a title described in the text.
      (RC) indicates a title with a Roman Catholic point of view.
      (E)   indicates a title with an evangelical or conservative point of view.

* * *

Outline

I. **General** (Reference sources useful for three or more courses)
  A. Religious Encyclopedias, Dictionaries, Handbooks
  B. Religious Bibliographies and Guides
  C. General Bibliographies and Guides
  D. Periodical Indexes and Abstracts
  E. Biography
  F. Book Reviews
  G. Quotations
  H. Thesaurus and Synonyms Book
  I. Style Manuals

II. **Bible**
  A. Encyclopedias, Dictionaries, and Handbooks
  B. Atlases
  C. Concordances
  D. Commentaries
  E. Bibliographies, Indexes, and Abstracts
  F. Apocryphal Literature
  G. Language Tools
    1. Hebrew
      a) Grammar
      b) Lexicons
      c) Concordances
      d) Interlinear Old Testament
    2. Greek
      a) Grammar
      b) Lexicons
      c) Concordances
      d) Interlinear New Testament

III. **Theology; Systematic Theology; Dogmatic Theology; Doctrinal Theology; Christian Beliefs**

IV. **Christian Ethics; Social Ethics; Moral Theology**

V. **Philosophy of Religion; Philosophical Theology**

VI. **Church History; History of Doctrine**

VII. **Worship; Preaching; Liturgy; Hymns**

VIII. **Christian Education; Religious Education; Audiovisual Resources; Group Leadership**

IX. **Religion and Psychology; Psychology of Religion; Pastoral Psychology; Pastoral Counseling**

X. **Sociology of Religion; Church and Society**

XI. **World Religions; Comparative Religion**
  A. General
  B. Buddhism
  C. Hinduism
  D. Islam
  E. Judaism

XII. **Roman Catholic Church**

XIII. **Eastern Orthodox Church**

XIV. **Denominations; Religion in the U.S.**

XV. **Ecumenics**

XVI. **Missions**

XVII. **Mythology and Folklore**

Answers to the Library Knowledge Test:
1. W. 2. Liberation through the Bible. 3. Yes. Bibliographical references are included. 4. a) Freedom (Theology)—Biblical teaching; b) Liberation theology; c) Topel, L. John. 5. The title is spelled out in the front of the *Readers' Guide.* 6. Page 84. 7. Volume 140. 8. Anonymous. 9. Front for the Liberation of Quebec. 10. Yes. ("il" is the abbreviation of "illustrated").

Since question four has three answers, a perfect score is 12. If you got only 7 or 8 correct, you probably need to spend time with the library guides mentioned in the Preface. If you got less than 7 correct answers, be sure to study those guides before proceeding with this book.

BIBLIOGRAPHY

I. GENERAL
(Reference sources useful for three or more courses)

A. Religious Encyclopedias, Dictionaries, and Handbooks

Baker's Dictionary of Practical Theology. Edited by Ralph B. Turnbull, Grand Rapids: Baker Book House, 1967, 469 pp.

(RC) *Encyclopedic Dictionary of Religion*. Edited by Paul K. Meagher and others. Philadelphia: Sisters of St. Joseph; Washington, DC: Corpus, 1979. 3 vols.

*Hastings, James, ed. *Encyclopedia of Religion and Ethics*. Edinburgh: Clark; New York: Scribner's, 1908-27. 12 vols. and index.

Magill, Frank N., ed. *Masterpieces of Christian Literature in Summary Form*. New York: Harper & Row, 1963. 1,193 pp.

(RC) *New Catholic Encyclopedia*. New York: McGraw-Hill, 1967. 15 vols. Supplements, 1974 and 1979.

New Schaff-Herzog Encyclopedia of Religious Knowledge. 1908-12. 12 vols. and index. Reprint. Grand Rapids: Baker, 1955. Supplemented by *Twentieth Century Encyclopedia of Religious Knowledge*. Grand Rapids: Baker Book House, 1955. 2 vols.

World Christian Encyclopedia. Edited by David B. Barrett. New York: Oxford University Press, 1982. 1,010 pp.

B. Religious Bibliographies and Guides

(E) Barber, Cyril J. *The Minister's Library*. Grand Rapids: Baker, 1974. 378 pp. *Volume 2, 1972-1980*, 1983. 224 pp. Volume 2 cumulates four supplements.

Bollier, John A. *The Literature of Theology; A Guide for Students and Pastors*. Philadelphia: Westminster, 1979. 208 pp.

(E) Branson, Mark L. *The Reader's Guide to the Best Evangelical Books*. San Francisco: Harper & Row, 1982. 207 pp.

Essential Books for a Pastor's Study; Basic and Recommended Works. 5th ed. Richmond, VA: Union Theological Seminary, 1976. 120 pp.

Kepple, Robert J. *Reference Works for Theological Research; An Annotated, Selective Bibliographical Guide*. 2nd ed.

Washington, DC: University Press of America, 1981. 283 pp. *Supplement*. Philadelphia: Westminster Theological Seminary, 1983. 27 pp.

(RC) McCabe, James Patrick. *Critical Guide to Catholic Reference Literature*. 2nd ed. Littleton, CO: Libraries Unlimited, 1980. 282 pp.

(E) Merchant, Harish, ed. *Encounter with Books; A Guide to Christian Reading*. Downers Grove, IL: Inter-Varsity, 1970. 292 pp.

Morris, Raymond P. *A Theological Book List*. London: The Theological Education Fund, 1960. Supplements, 1963, 1968, and 1972, compiled by A. Marcus Ward and others.

Religion Index Two; Multi-Author Works, 1970-1975. Chicago: American Theological Library Association, 1982. 2 vols. *1976-- . 1978-- . Annual.

Religious Books, 1876-1982. New York: Bowker, 1983. 4 vols.

Religious Books and Serials in Print, 1982-1983. New York: Bowker, 1982. 1,524 pp.

Southwestern Baptist Theological Seminary, Fleming Library Staff. *Essential Books for Christian Ministry; Basic Reading for Pastors, Church Staff Leaders, and Laymen*. Fort Worth, TX: Southwestern Baptist Theological Seminary, 1972. 128 pp.

C. General Bibliographies and Guides

Ash, Lee. *Subject Collections; A Guide to Special Book Collections and Subject Emphases*. 5th ed. New York: Bowker, 1978. 1,184 pp.

Bibliographic Index; A Cumulative Bibliography of Bibliographies. New York: Wilson, 1938-- . Two times a year, with annual cumulations.

Books for College Libraries; A Core Collection of 40,000 Titles. 2nd ed. Chicago: American Library Association, 1975. 6 vols.

Dissertation Abstracts International; Abstracts of Dissertations Available on Microfilm or as Xerographic Reproductions. Ann Arbor: Xerox University Microfilms, 1938-- . Monthly. In 2 parts beginning with July, 1966. Part A covers the humanities and social sciences.

Essay and General Literature Index 1900-33. Edited by M. E. Sears and M. Shaw. New York: Wilson, 1934. Supplements. New York: Wilson, 1937-- . Semiannual with annual and five-year cumulations.

Library of Congress. *Library of Congress Catalog — Books: Subjects; A Cumulative List of Works Represented by Library of Congress Printed Cards*, 1950-- . Washington: Library of Congress, 1955-- .

Library of Congress, Subject Cataloging Division. *Library of Congress Subject Headings*. 9th ed. Washington: Library of Congress, 1980. *Supplements*, 1980-- .

National Union Catalog; A Cumulative Author List, 1956-- . Washington: Library of Congress, 1958-- . Monthly with quarterly, annual and five-year cumulations. Preceded by: Library of Congress. *A Catalog of Books Represented by the Library of Congress Printed Cards, Issued to July 1942*. Ann Arbor: Edwards, 1942-46. 167 vols. Supplemented by later cumulations.

National Union Catalog, Pre-1956 Imprints . . . London: Mansell, 1968-1980. 685 vols. *Supplement*. 1980-- .

*Walford, A.J. *Walford's Guide to Reference Material*. 4th ed. London: The Library Association, 1980-- .

Sheehy, Eugene P. *Guide to Reference Books*. 9th ed. Chicago: American Library Association, 1976. Supplements, 1980-- .

D. Periodical Indexes and Abstracts

Catholic Periodical and Literature Index. Haverford, PA: Catholic Library Association, 1930-- . Bimonthly with two-year cumulations.

(E) *Christian Periodical Index, 1956--* . Buffalo: Christian Librarians' Fellowship, 1961-- . Quarterly with annual and three-year cumulations.

Humanities Index, 1974-- . New York: Wilson, 1975-- . Quarterly with annual cumulations. (Entitled *Social Sciences & Humanities Index* from 1965 to 1975 and *International Index* from 1907 to 1965.)

Nineteenth Century Readers' Guide to Periodical Literature, 1890-99, with Supplementary Indexing 1900-22. New York: Wilson, 1944. 2 vols.

Poole's Index to Periodical Literature, 1802-1906. Vol. 1, 1802-81, Boston: Osgood, 1882; vols. 2-6, Boston: Houghton, 1888-1908.

Readers' Guide to Periodical Literature, 1900-- . New York: Wilson, 1905-- . Bimonthly with quarterly and annual cumulations.

Regazzi, John J., and Hines, Theodore C. *A Guide to Indexed Periodicals in Religion*. Metuchen, NJ: Scarecrow, 1975. 314 pp.

Religion Index One: Periodicals; A Subject Index to Periodical Literature, Including an Author Index, with Abstracts, and a Book Review Index. Chicago: American Theological Library Association, 1949-- . Semiannual with two-year cumulations. Quarterly on microfiche. Entitled *Index to Religious Periodical Literature* before 1977.

Religion Indexes: Thesaurus. 2nd ed. Chicago: American Theological Library Association, Religion Indexes, 1983. 268 pp.

Religious and Theological Abstracts. Myerstown, PA: Religious and Theological Abstracts, 1958-- . Quarterly.

Social Sciences Index, 1974-- . New York: Wilson, 1975-- . Quarterly with annual cumulations. (Entitled *Social Sciences & Humanities Index* from 1965 to 1975 and *International Index* from 1907 to 1965.)

E. Biography

Biography and Genealogy Master Index, 2nd ed., 8 vols. (Detroit: Gale, 1980); *Supplement, 1981-82*, 3 vols., 1982.

Biography Index. New York: Wilson, 1946-- . Quarterly with annual and three-year cumulations.

Contemporary Authors; A Bio-Bibliographical Guide to Current Authors and Their Works. Detroit: Gale, 1962-- .

Directory of American Scholars. Edited by Jaques Cattell Press. 8th ed. New York: Bowker, 1982. 4 vols.

Who Was Who. London: Black, 1935-- . Vols. 1-7, 1935-81, cover 1897--1980.

Who Was Who in America. Chicago: Marquis-Who's Who, 1942-- . Vols. 1-8, 1942-76, cover 1607-1976.

*Who's Who. New York: St. Martin's Press, 1849-- . Annual.

*Who's Who in America. Chicago: Marquis-Who's Who, 1899-- . Biennial.

Who's Who in Religion, 1977-78. 2nd ed. Chicago: Marquis-Who's Who, 1977. 736 pp.

F. Book Reviews

Book Reviews of the Month; An Index to Reviews Appearing in Selected Theological Journals. Fort Worth, TX: Fleming Library, Southwestern Baptist Theological Seminary, 1962-- . Monthly with annual cumulations.

Book Review Digest. New York: Wilson, 1905-- . Monthly with quarterly and annual cumulations.

Book Review Index. Detroit: Gale, 1965-- . Bimonthly with quarterly and annual cumulations.

An Index to Book Reviews in the Humanities. Detroit: Thomson, 1960-- . Annual.

G. Quotations

Baron, Joseph Louis, ed. *A Treasury of Jewish Quotations*. Rev. ed. South Brunswick, NJ: Yoseloff, 1965. 623 pp.

(RC) Chapin, John. *The Book of Catholic Quotations; Compiled from Approved Sources, Ancient, Medieval, and Modern*. New York: Farrar, Straus and Cudahy, 1956. 1,073 pp.

Mead, Frank Spencer, ed. and comp. *Encyclopedia of Religious Quotations*. Westwood, NJ: Revell, 1965. 534 pp.

Rosten, Leo Calvin. *Leo Rosten's Treasury of Jewish Quotations*. New York: McGraw-Hill, 1972. 716 pp.

Simcox, Carroll E., comp. *A Treasury of Quotations on Christian Themes*. New York: Seabury, 1975. 269 pp.

*Stevenson, Burton. *Home Book of Quotations*. 10th ed. New York: Dodd Mead, 1967. 2,816 pp.

Wirt, Sherwood Eliot, and Beckstrom, Kersten, comp. and ed. *Topical Encyclopedia of Living Quotations*. Minneapolis: Bethany, 1982. 290 pp. Revised edition of *Living Quotations for Christians*, 1974.

*Woods, Ralph L. *The World Treasury of Religious Quotations*. New York: Hawthorn, 1966. 1,106 pp.

H. Thesaurus and Synonyms Book

Rodale, Jerome I. *The Synonym Finder*. Rev. ed. Emmaus, PA: Rodale, 1978. 1,361 pp.

Roget's International Thesaurus. 4th ed. New York: Crowell, 1977. 1,317 pp.

I. Style Manuals

Turabian, Kate L. *A Manual for Writers of Term Papers, Theses, and Dissertations*. 4th ed., rev. Chicago: University of Chicago Press, 1973. 216 pp.

University of Chicago Press. *The Chicago Manual of Style*. 13th ed. Chicago: University of Chicago Press, 1982. 738 pp.

II. BIBLE

A. Encyclopedias, Dictionaries, and Handbooks

(E) Allison, Joseph D. *The Bible Study Resource Guide*. Nashville: Nelson, 1982. 223 pp.

Bailey, Lloyd R. *The Word of God; A Guide to English Versions of the Bible*. Atlanta: John Knox, 1982. 228 pp.

(RC) Bauer, Johannes Baptist, ed. *Sacramentum Verbi; An Encyclopedia of Biblical Theology*. New York: Herder and Herder, 1970. 3 vols. Reprinted as: *Encyclopedia of Biblical Theology*. 1981.

Botterweck, G. Johannes, and Ringgren, Helmer, eds. *Theological Dictionary of the Old Testament*. Grand Rapids: Eerdmans, 1974. Vols. 1-4, 1974-1980, cover "abh" to "hms."

The Cambridge History of the Bible. Edited by P.R. Ackroyd and others. Cambridge: Cambridge University Press, 1963-70. 3 vols.

Catholic Biblical Encyclopedia; Old and New Testaments, by John E. Steinmueller and Kathryn Sullivan. New York: Wagner, 1956. 2 vols. in 1.

Cully, Iris V., and Cully, Kendig Brubaker. *A Guide to Biblical Resources*. Wilton, CT: Morehouse-Barlow, 1981. 153 pp.

*Danker, Frederick W. *Multipurpose Tools for Bible Study*. 3rd ed. St. Louis: Concordia, 1970. 295 pp.

(E) Douglas, James Dixon, ed. *The New Bible Dictionary*. 2nd ed. Wheaton, IL: Tyndale, 1982. 1,326 pp.

Encyclopaedia Judaica. Edited by Cecil Roth and Geoffrey Wigoder. Jerusalem: Encyclopaedia Judaica, Macmillan, 1971. 16 vols.

Encyclopedia of Archaeological Excavations in the Holy Land. English edition edited by Michael Avi-Yonah. Englewood Cliffs, NJ: Prentice-Hall, 1975-1978. 4 vols.

(E) Fee, Gordon D. *New Testament Exegesis; A Handbook for Students and Pastors*. Philadelphia: Westminster, 1983. 154 pp.

*Gehman, Henry Snyder. *The Westminster Dictionary of the Bible*. Philadelphia: Westminster, 1970. 1,027 pp.

*Grant, Frederick C., and Rowley, H.H. *Dictionary of the Bible*. Rev. ed. New York: Scribner's, 1963. 1,059 pp.

Guides to Biblical Scholarship. Edited by Gene M. Tucker. Philadelphia: Fortress, 1971-- . Seventeen volumes were published before 1984.

(E) *The Illustrated Bible Dictionary*. Wheaton, IL: Tyndale House, 1980. 3 vols.

*(E) *The International Standard Bible Encyclopedia*. Edited by Geoffrey W. Bromiley. Rev. ed. Grand Rapids: Eerdmans, 1979-- . Vols. 1-2, 1979-1982, cover "A" to "J."

The Interpreter's Dictionary of the Bible. New York: Abingdon, 1962. 4 vols. *Supplementary Volume*, 1976.

*Kittel, Gerhard, ed. *Theological Dictionary of the New Testament*. Grand Rapids: Eerdmans, 1964-76. 10 vols. Primarily for advanced students.

(RC) Leon-Dufour, Xavier. *Dictionary of the New Testament*. Translated from the 2nd French edition. New York: Harper & Row, 1980. 458 pp.

Lewis, Jack P. *The English Bible, from KJV to NIV; A History and Evaluation*. Grand Rapids: Baker, 1981. 408 pp.

(RC) McKenzie, John Lawrence. *Dictionary of the Bible*. Milwaukee: Bruce, 1965. 954 pp.

Miller, Madeleine Sweeney, and Miller, J. Lane. *Harper's Bible Dictionary*. 8th ed. New York: Harper & Row, 1973. 853 pp. Identical to *Black's Bible Dictionary*, 1973.

Negev, Avraham, ed. *Archaeological Encyclopedia of the Holy Land*. New York: Putnam's, 1972. 354 pp.

(E) *The New International Dictionary of New Testament Theology; Translated, with Additions and Revisions, from the German Theologisches Begriffslexikon zum Neuen Testament*. Edited by Colin Brown, Grand

Rapids: Zondervan, 1975-78. 3 vols.

Orr, James, and others, ed. *International Standard Bible Encyclopedia*. Rev. ed. Grand Rapids: Eerdmans, 1930. 5 vols.

Richardson, Alan, ed. *A Theological Word Book of the Bible*. New York: Macmillan, 1950. 290 pp.

Soulen, Richard N. *Handbook of Biblical Criticism*. 2nd ed. Atlanta: John Knox, 1981. 239 pp.

Stuart, Douglas. *Old Testament Exegesis; A Primer for Students and Pastors*. Philadelphia: Westminster, 1980. 143 pp.

Theological Wordbook of the Old Testament. Edited by R. Laird Harris and others. Chicago: Moody, 1980. 2 vols.

(E) *The Zondervan Pictorial Encyclopedia of the Bible*. Edited by Merrill C. Tenney. Grand Rapids: Zondervan, 1975. 5 vols.

B. Atlases

Aharoni, Yohanan, and Avi-Yonah, Michael. *The Macmillan Bible Atlas*. Rev. ed. New York: Macmillan, 1977. 184 pp. Only slightly different from the first edition, 1968.

Grollenberg, Luc H. *Atlas of the Bible*. London: Nelson, 1963. 165 pp.

Pfeiffer, Charles. *Baker's Bible Atlas*. Rev. ed. Grand Rapids: Baker, 1979. 340 pp.

The Westminster Historical Atlas to the Bible. Edited by George Ernest Wright and Floyd V. Filson. Rev. ed. Philadelphia: Westminster, 1956. 130 pp.

C. Concordances

*Cruden, Alexander. *Cruden's Complete Concordance to the Old and New Testaments*. 1738. Reprint. Grand Rapids: Zondervan, 1968. 803 pp.

Ellison, John, ed. *Nelson's Complete Concordance of the Revised Standard Version Bible*. 2nd ed. Nashville: Nelson, 1972. 2,157 pp.

(E) Goodrick, Edward W., and Kohlenberger, John R., III. *The NIV Complete Concordance; The Complete English Concordance to the New International Version*. Grand Rapids: Zondervan, 1981. 1,044 pp.

(RC) *Nelson's Complete Concordance of the New American Bible*. Edited by Stephen J. Hartdegen. Nashville:

Nelson, 1977. 1,274 pp.

Morrison, Clinton. *An Analytical Concordance to the Revised Standard Version of the New Testament*. Philadelphia: Westminster, 1979. 773 pp.

New American Standard Exhaustive Concordance of the Bible. Edited by Robert L. Thomas. Nashville: Holman, 1981. 1,695 pp.

Speer, Jack Atkeson, ed. and comp. *The Living Bible Concordance, Complete*. Poolesville, MD: Poolesville Presbyterian Church, 1973. 1,209 pp.

Strong, James. *The Exhaustive Concordance of the Bible; with a Key-Word Comparison of Selected Words and Phrases in the King James Version with Five Leading Contemporary Translations*. Nashville: Abingdon, 1980. Various paging.

*Young, Robert. *Analytical Concordance to the Bible* . . . . 22nd American ed; New York: Funk & Wagnalls, 1955. 1,090 pp.

D. Commentaries (mostly in several volumes)

The Anchor Bible. Garden City, NY: Doubleday, 1964-- .

(RC) Brown, Raymond E., and others. *The Jerome Biblical Commentary*. Englewood Cliffs, NJ: Prentice-Hall, 1968. 637 pp. and 889 pp.

(E) Guthrie, Donald, and Motyer, J.A., eds. *The New Bible Commentary, Revised*. 3rd ed. Grand Rapids: Eerdmans, 1970. 1,310 pp.

Harper's New Testament Commentaries. New York: Harper & Row, 1957-- .

Hermeneia; A Critical and Historical Commentary on the Bible Series. Philadelphia: Fortress, 1971-- . Primarily for advanced students.

International Critical Commentary on the Holy Scriptures. Edited by S.R. Driver and others. 2nd ed. Edinburgh: Clark, 1930. 46 vols. A new edition began in 1975.

Interpretation; A Bible Commentary for Teaching and Preaching. Atlanta: John Knox, 1982-- . Three volumes were published before 1984.

The Interpreter's Bible. Edited by George A. Buttrick and others. Nashville: Abingdon-Cokesbury, 1953-56. 12 vols.

The Interpreter's One-Volume Commentary on the Bible;

Introduction and Commentary for Each Book of the Bible, Including Apocrypha; with General Articles. Edited by Charles M. Laymon. Nashville: Abingdon, 1971. 1,386 pp.

New Century Bible; Based on the Revised Standard Version. Grand Rapids: Eerdmans, 1966-- . Twenty-five volumes were published before 1984.

New International Commentary on the New Testament. Grand Rapids: Eerdmans, 1954-- .

The New International Commentary on the Old Testament. Edited by R.K. Harrison. Grand Rapids: Eerdmans, 1965-- . Fifteen volumes were published before 1984.

Old Testament Library. Philadelphia: Westminster, 1961-- .

(E) *Tyndale New Testament Commentaries*. Edited by Randolph Vincent Greenwood Trasker. Grand Rapids: Eerdmans, 1957-1974. 20 vols.

(E) *The Tyndale Old Testament Commentaries*. Edited by D.J. Wiseman. London: Inter-Varsity Fellowship, 1974-- . Fourteen volumes published before 1984.

(E) *The Wesleyan Bible Commentary*. Grand Rapids: Eerdmans, 1964-1969. 6 vols.

E. Bibliographies, Indexes, and Abstracts

(E) Allison, Joseph D. *The Bible Study Resource Guide*. Nashville: Nelson, 1982. 223 pp.

Barker, Kenneth L., and Waltke, Bruce K. *Bibliography for Old Testament Exegesis and Exposition*. 4th ed. Dallas: Dallas Theological Seminary, 1979. 73 pp.

Charlesworth, James H. *The Pseudepigrapha and Modern Research, with a Supplement*. Chico, CA: Published by Scholars Press for the Society of Biblical Literature, 1981. 329 pp.

Childs, Brevard S. *Old Testament Books for Pastor and Teacher*. Philadelphia: Westminster, 1977. 120 pp.

*Clifford E. Barbour Library. *A Periodical and Monographic Index to the Literature on the Gospels and Acts*. Pittsburgh: Pittsburgh Theological Seminary, Clifford E. Barbour Library, 1971. 336 pp.

Elenchus Bibliographicus Biblicus. Rome: Biblical Institute Press, 1920-- . Annual. The most comprehensive current bibliography on biblical studies. Published as part of the periodical *Biblica* until 1968.

Fitzmyer, Joseph A. *The Dead Sea Scrolls: Major Publications and Tools for Study; with an Addendum (January 1977)*. Missoula, MT: Scholars, 1977. 177 pp., 5 pp.

(RC) Fitzmyer, Joseph A. *Introductory Bibliography for the Study of Scripture*. Rev. ed. Rome: Biblical Institute Press, 1981. 154 pp.

France, R.T. *A Bibliographical Guide to New Testament Research*. 3rd ed. Sheffield, England: J.S.O.T. Press, 1979. 56 pp.

(RC) Fitzmyer, Joseph A. *An Introductory Bibliography for the Study of Scripture*. Rev. ed. Rome: Biblical Institute Press, 1981. 154 pp.

Gottcent, John H. *The Bible as Literature; A Selective Bibliography*. Boston: Hall, 1979. 170 pp.

Hurd, John Coolidge, Jr., comp. *A Bibliography of New Testament Bibliographies*. New York: Seabury, 1966. 75 pp.

Internationale Zeitschriftenschau fuer Bibelwissenschaft und Grenzegebiete; International Review of Biblical Studies. Stuttgart: Katholisches Bibelwerk, 1951-- . Annual. Primarily abstracts of foreign language materials.

Kissinger, Warren S. *The Parables of Jesus; A History of Interpretation and Bibliography*. Metuchen, NJ: Scarecrow, 1979. 439 pp.

Kissinger, Warren S. *The Sermon on the Mount; A History of Interpretation and Bibliography*. Metuchen, NJ: Scarecrow, 1975. 296 pp.

Marrow, Stanley B. *Basic Tools for Biblical Exegesis*. Rome: Biblical Institute Press, 1976. 91 pp.

*Mattill, A.J., and Mattill, Nancy Bedford. *A Classified Bibliography of Literature on the Acts of the Apostles*. Grand Rapids: Eerdmans, 1966. 513 pp.

*Metzger, Bruce M. *Index to Periodical Literature on Christ and the Gospels*. Grand Rapids: Eerdmans, 1966. 602 pp.

*Metzger, Bruce M. *Index to Periodical Literature on the Apostle Paul*. Grand Rapids: Eerdmans, 1960. 183 pp.

New Testament Abstracts. Cambridge, MA: Weston College School of Theology, 1956-- . Three times a year.

Old Testament Abstracts. Washington, DC: Catholic University of America, 1978-- . Three times a year.

Scholer, David M. *A Basic Bibliographic Guide for New*

Testament Exegesis. 2nd ed. Grand Rapids: Eerdmans, 1973. 94 pp.

Vogel, Eleanor K., comp. *Bibliography of Holy Land Sites*. Cincinnati: Hebrew Union College--Jewish Institute of Religion, 1972. 96 pp. *Part II (1970-1981)*. 1982. 92 pp.

F. Apocryphal Literature

Bible. New Testament. Apocryphal Books. English, 1963. *New Testament Apocrypha*. Edited by Edgar Hennecke and Wilhelm Schneemelcher. Philadelphia: Westminster, 1963-66. 2 vols.

Bible. Old Testament. Apocrypha and Apocryphal Books. English. 1913. *The Apocrypha and Pseudepigrapha of the Old Testament in English*. Edited by R.H. Charles. Oxford: Clarendon, 1913. 2 vols.

A Concordance to the Apocrypha/Deuterocanonical Books of the Revised Standard Version. Grand Rapids: Eerdmans, 1983. 479 pp.

The Old Testament Pseudepigrapha. Edited by James H. Charlesworth. Garden City, NY: Doubleday, 1983-- . Vol. 1 entitled *Apocryphal Literature and Testaments*.

G. Language Tools

1. Hebrew

a) Grammar

Gesenius, Friedrich Heinrich Wilhelm. *Gesenius' Hebrew Grammar*. Edited and enlarged by E. Kautzsch. 2nd English ed. revised by A.E. Cowley, Oxford: Clarendon, 1910. 598 pp.

b) Lexicons

Armstrong, Terry A., and others. *A Reader's Hebrew-English Lexicon of the Old Testament*. Grand Rapids: Zondervan, 1980. 146 pp. Vols. 1 and 2, 1980-82 cover Genesis to 2 Kings.

Einspahr, Bruce, comp. *Index to Brown, Driver & Briggs Hebrew Lexicon*. Chicago: Moody, 1976. 452 pp.

Gesenius, Friedrich Heinrich Wilhelm. *A Hebrew and English Lexicon of the Old Testament with an Appendix Containing the Biblical Aramaic, Based on the Lexicon of William Gesenius as Translated by Edward Robinson*. Edited by Francis Brown, S.R. Driver, and Charles A. •

Briggs. Boston: Houghton, Mifflin, 1906. 1,127 pp. (Often called Brown, Driver and Briggs.)

Holladay, William L. *A Concise Hebrew and Aramaic Lexicon of the Old Testament*. Grand Rapids: Eerdmans, 1972. 425 pp. An English language abridgment of Koehler's *Hebraeisches und Aramaeisches Lexikon zum Alten Testament*.

Koehler, Ludwig Hugo, *Hebraeisches und aramaisches Lexikon zum Alten Testament*. 3rd ed. revised by Walter Baumgartner. Leiden, Netherlands: Brill, 1967-- . Previously entitled *Lexicon in Veteris Testamenti Libros*.

The New Brown, Driver and Briggs Hebrew and English Lexicon of the Old Testament; Based on the Lexicon of William Gesenius. Edited by Francis Brown, S.R. Driver and Charles A. Briggs. Lafayette, IN: Associated Publishers and Authors, 1981, c1907. 1,118 pp. and 58 pp.

Theological Wordbook of the Old Testament. Edited by R. Laird Harris and others. Chicago: Moody, 1980. 2 vols.

c) Concordances

Mandelkern, Salomon. *Veteris Testamenti Concordantiae Hebraicae atque Chaldaicae . . . .* 3rd ed. (?) Tel Aviv: Schocken, 1967. 1,565 pp.

Lisowsky, Gerhard. *Konkordanz zum Hebraeischen Alten Testament . . . .* 2nd ed. Stuttgart: Privilegierte Wuerttembergische Bibelanstalt, 1981. 1,672 pp.

d) Interlinear Old Testament

Bible. O.T. Hebrew. 1979. *The NIV Interlinear Hebrew-English Old Testament*. Edited by John R. Kohlenberger III. Grand Rapids: Zondervan, 1979-- . Vols. 1-3, 1979-1982, cover Genesis to Song of Songs.

2. *Greek*

a) Grammar

Blass, Friedrich Wilhelm and Debrunner, A. *A Greek Grammar of the New Testament and Other Early Christian Literature*. Chicago: University of Chicago Press, 1961. 325 pp.

Moulton, James Hope. *A Grammar of New Testament Greek*. Edinburgh: Clark, 1909-76. 4 vols.

Rienecker, Fritz. *A Linguistic Key to the Greek New Testament; Translated with Additions and Revisions from the German Sprachlicher Schluessel zum griechischen Neuen Testament*. Grand Rapids: Zondervan, 1976-1980. 2 vols.

b) Lexicons

Alsop, John R., ed. *An Index to the Revised Bauer-Arndt-Gingrich Greek Lexicon*. 2nd ed. By F. Wilbur Gingrich and Frederick W. Danker. Grand Rapids: Zondervan, 1981. 525 pp.

Arndt, William, and Gingrich, F. *A Greek-English Lexicon of the New Testament and Other Early Christian Literature*. 2nd ed. Chicago: University of Chicago Press, 1979. 900 pp.

Kubo, Sakae. *A Reader's Greek-English Lexicon of the New Testament and a Beginner's Guide for the Translation of New Testament Greek*. Grand Rapids: Zondervan, 1975. 327 pp.

Liddell, Henry George, and Scott, Robert. *Greek-English Lexicon . . . . A New Edition Revised and Augmented Throughout* by Henry Stuart Jones. 9th ed. Oxford: Clarendon, 1925-40. 1,776 pp. *A Supplement*. Oxford: Clarendon, 1968. 153 pp.

c) Concordances

Computer-Konkordanz zum Novum Testamentum Graecae von Nestle-Aland. 3rd ed. Berlin; New York: De Gruyter, 1980. 1,964 columns and 64 columns.

Hatch, Edwin, and Redpath, Henry A. *A Concordance to the Septuagint and the Other Greek Versions of the Old Testament (including the Apocryphal Books)*. Oxford: Clarendon, 1897-1906. 2 vols. and supplement.

Moulton, William F. *A Concordance to the Greek Testament*. 5th ed. Edinburgh: Clark, 1978. 1,110 pp.

d) Interlinear New Testament

Bible, N.T. Greek. 1968. *The R.S.V. Interlinear Greek-English New Testament; The Nestle*

Greek Text with a Literal English Translation by Alfred Marshall... Also a Marginal Text of the Revised Standard Version. Grand Rapids: Zondervan, 1968. 1,027 pp.

III. THEOLOGY; SYSTEMATIC THEOLOGY; DOGMATIC THEOLOGY: DOCTRINAL THEOLOGY; CHRISTIAN BELIEFS

A. Encyclopedias, Dictionaries, and Handbooks

(E) *Baker's Dictionary of Theology*. Edited by Everett F. Harrison, Geoffrey W. Bromiley, and Carl F.H. Henry. Grand Rapids: Baker Book House, 1960. 566 pp.

Davis, John Jefferson. *Theology Primer; Resources for the Theological Student*. Grand Rapids: Baker, 1981. 111 pp.

The Encyclopedia of Philosophy. Edited by Paul Edwards. New York: Macmillan, 1967. 8 vols.

Harvey, Van A. *A Handbook of Theological Terms*. New York: Macmillan, 1966. 217 pp.

(RC) Leon-DuFour, Xavier, ed. *Dictionary of Biblical Theology*. 2nd ed. London: G. Chapman, 1973. 711 pp.

Rahner, Karl, and Vorgrimler, Herbert. *Dictionary of Theology*. 2nd ed. New York: Crossroad, 1981. 541 pp.

(RC) *Rahner, Karl, and others, eds. *Sacramentum Mundi; An Encyclopedia of Theology*. New York: Herder & Herder, 1968-70. 6 vols.

Ramm, Bernard, ed. *A Handbook of Contemporary Theology*. Grand Rapids: Eerdmans, 1966. 141 pp.

Richardson, Alan and Bowden, John, eds. *A New Dictionary of Christian Theology*. London: SCM, 1983. 614 pp.

Ziefle, Helmut W. *Dictionary of Modern Theological German*. Grand Rapids: Baker, 1982. 199 pp.

B. Bibliographies

Ephemerides Theologicae Lovanienses. "Elenchus Bibliographicus." Louvain: Universite Catholique, 1924-- . Annual. The most comprehensive current bibliography of theology.

Princeton Theological Seminary, Library. *A Bibliography of Systematic Theology for Theological Students*. Princeton. NJ: Princeton Theological Seminary, Library, 1949. 44 pp.

IV. CHRISTIAN ETHICS; SOCIAL ETHICS; MORAL THEOLOGY

Anglemyer, Mary, and others. *A Search for Environmental Ethics; An Initial Bibliography*. Washington, DC: Smithsonian Institution Press, 1980. 119 pp.

Baker's Dictionary of Christian Ethics. Edited by Carl F. Henry. Grand Rapids: Baker, 1973. 726 pp.

Bibliography of Bioethics. Edited by LeRoy Walters. New York: Free Press, 1975-- . Annual. (Volumes 1-6 published by Gale.)

Carroll, Berenice A., and others. *Peace and War; A Guide to Bibliographies*. Santa Barbara, CA: ABC-Clio, 1983. 580 pp.

Encyclopedia of Bioethics. Edited by Warren T. Reich. New York: Free Press, 1978. 4 vols.

Goldstein, Doris Mueller. *Bioethics; A Guide to Information Sources*. Detroit: Gale, 1982. 366 pp.

Jones, Donald G., and Troy, Helen. *A Bibliography of Business Ethics, 1971-1975*. Charlottesville, VA: University Press of Virginia, 1977. 207 pp. *1976-1980*. 1982. 220 pp.

Leming, James S. *Contemporary Approaches to Moral Education; An Annotated Bibliography and Guide to Research*. New York: Garland, 1983. 451 pp.

Macquarrie, John, ed. *Dictionary of Christian Ethics*. Philadelphia: Westminster, 1967. 366 pp.

(RC) Roberti, Francesco. *Dictionary of Moral Theology*. Westminster, MD: Newman, 1962. 1,352 pp.

V. PHILOSOPHY OF RELIGION; PHILOSOPHICAL THEOLOGY

A. Encyclopedias, Dictionaries, and Handbooks

Dictionary of the History of Ideas; Studies of Selected Pivotal Ideas. Edited by Philip P. Wiener. New York: Scribner's, 1973-74. 5 vols.

Eliade, Mircea. *A History of Religious Ideas*. Translated from the French. Chicago, IL: University of Chicago Press, 1978-- . Vols. 1 and 2, 1978 and 1982 cover from the Stone Age to the triumph of Christianity.

The Encyclopedia of Philosophy. Edited by Paul Edwards. New York: Macmillan and Free Press, 1967. 8 vols.

Flew, Antony, ed. *A Dictionary of Philosophy*. New York: St. Martin's, 1979. 351 pp.

The Great Ideas; A Syntopicon of Great Books of the Western World. Chicago: W. Benton, 1952. 2 vols. (Great Books of the Western World, vols. 2, 3.)

Reese, William L. *Dictionary of Philosophy and Religion; Eastern and Western Thought.* Atlantic Highlands, NJ: Humanities, 1980. 644 pp.

B. Bibliographies and Indexes

Bibliographie de la Philosophie; Bibliography of Philosophy. Paris: J. Vrin, 1954-- . Quarterly.

DeGeorge, Richard T. *A Guide to Philosophical Bibliography and Research.* New York: Appleton-Century-Crofts, 1971. 141 pp.

Guerry, Herbert. *A Bibliography of Philosophical Bibliographies.* Westport, CT: Greenwood, 1977. 332 pp.

Jordak, Francis Elliott. *A Bibliographical Survey for a Foundation in Philosophy.* Washington, DC: University Press of America, 1978. 435 pp.

(RC) McLean, George F., ed. *An Annotated Bibliography of Philosophy in Catholic Thought, 1900-1964.* New York: Ungar, 1967. 371 pp.

(RC) McLean, George F., ed. *A Bibliography of Christian Philosophy and Contemporary Issues.* New York: Ungar, 1967. 312 pp.

The Philosopher's Index. Bowling Green, OH: Bowling Green University Press, 1968-- . Quarterly with annual cumulations. *The Philosopher's Index; A Retrospective Index to U.S. Publications from 1940.* 1978. 3 vols. *The Philosopher's Index; A Retrospective Index to Non-U.S. English Language Publications from 1940.* 1980. 3 vols.

Wainwright, William J. *Philosophy of Religion; An Annotated Bibliography of Twentieth-Century Writings in English.* New York: Garland, 1978. 776 pp. Limited to works by analytic philosophers.

VI. CHURCH HISTORY; HISTORY OF DOCTRINE

A. Encyclopedias, Dictionaries, Handbooks, and Histories

Altaner, Berthold. *Patrology.* New York: Herder and Herder, 1960. 659 pp.

Brauer, Jerald C., ed. *The Westminster Dictionary of Church History.* Philadelphia: Westminster, 1971. 887 pp.

Dictionary of the Middle Ages. Edited by Joseph R. Strayer. New York: Scribner's, 1982-- . Vols. 1 to 3, 1982 to 1983, cover "Aachon" to "Crimea."

(E) Douglas, James Dixon, ed. *The New International Dictionary of the Christian Church.* Grand Rapids: Zondervan, 1974. 1,074 pp.

(RC) *History of the Church.* Edited by Hubert Jedin and John Dolan. New York: Crossroad, 1980-1981. 10 vols. (Translated from the third German edition.)

Latourette, Kenneth Scott. *A History of the Expansion of Christianity.* New York: Harper, 1937-45. 7 vols.

Littell, Franklin H. *The Macmillan Atlas History of Christianity.* New York: Macmillan, 1976. 176 pp.

(E) Moyer, Elgin. *The Wycliffe Biographical Dictionary of the Church.* Revised and enlarged by Earle E. Cairns. Chicago: Moody Press, 1982. 449 pp.

O'Brien, Thomas C., ed. *Corpus Dictionary of the Western Churches.* Washington, DC: Corpus, 1970. 848 pp.

The Oxford Dictionary of the Christian Church. Edited by Frank L. Cross and E.A. Livingston. 2nd ed. London, New York, and Toronto: Oxford University Press, 1974. 1,518 pp.

Walker, Williston. *A History of the Christian Church.* 3rd ed., revised by Robert T. Handy. New York: Scribner's, 1970. 601 pp.

B. Bibliographies

Bainton, Roland H., and Gritsch, Eric W. *Bibliography of the Continentals Reformation: Materials Available in English.* 2nd ed. Hamden, CT: Archon, 1972. 220 pp.

Boyce, Gray Cowan. *Literature of Medieval History, 1930-1975; A Supplement to Louis John Paetow's "A Guide to the Study of Medieval History."* Millwood, NY: Kraus, 1981. 5 vols.

Case, Shirley J., and others, comp. *A Bibliographical Guide to the History of Christianity.* Chicago: University of Chicago Press, 1931. 265 pp.

Chadwick, Owen. *The History of the Church, A Select Bibliography.* 3rd ed. London: Historical Association, 1973. 52 pp.

Paetow, Louis John. *A Guide to the Study of Medieval History.* Rev. ed. New York: Crofts, 1931. 643 pp.

Revue d'histoire Ecclesiastique. "Bibliographie." Louvain: Universite Catholique de Louvain, 1900-- . Annual. The most comprehensive current bibliography of church history.

C. Documents, Collections, and Readings

Ancient Christian Writers; The Works of the Fathers in Translation. Edited by Johannes Quasten and others. Westminster, MD: Newman, 1946-75. 40 vols.

Bettenson, Henry S., ed. *Documents of the Christian Church.* 2nd ed. London, New York, and Toronto: Oxford University Press, 1963. 489 pp.

The Fathers of the Church; A New Translation. Washington, DC: Catholic University of America Press, 1947-- . 71 vols. published before 1984.

Library of Christian Classics. Edited by John Baillie and others. Philadelphia: Westminster, 1953-69. 26 vols.

VII. WORSHIP; PREACHING; LITURGY; HYMNS

Bowman, Mary Ann, comp. *Western Mysticism; A Guide to the Basic Works.* Chicago: American Library Association, 1978. 113 pp.

Davies, J.G., ed. *A Dictionary of Liturgy and Worship.* New York: Macmillan, 1972. 385 pp. Reprinted in 1979 as *The Westminster Dictionary of Worship.*

Diehl, Katherine Smith. *Hymns and Tunes; An Index.* New York: Scarecrow, 1966. 1,185 pp.

Fant, Clyde E., and Pinson, William M. *20 Centuries of Great Preaching; An Encyclopedia of Preaching.* Waco, TX: Word, 1971. 13 vols.

Garland, George Frederick, comp. *Subject Guide to Bible Stories.* New York: Greenwood, 1969. 365 pp.

(RC) Herrera Oria, Angel, Cardinal. *The Preacher's Encyclopedia.* Westminster, MD: Newman, 1964-65. 4 vols.

(RC) Kiefer, William J., ed. *Biblical Subject Index.* Westminster, MD: Newman, 1958. 197 pp.

Nicoll, W. Robertson, and Stoddart, Jane T. *The Expositor's Dictionary of Texts; Containing Outlines, Expositions, and Illustrations of Bible Texts, with Full References to the Best Homiletical Literature.* London: Hodder and Stoughton, 1910-11. 2 vols.

Recent Homiletical Thought; A Bibliography, 1935-65. Edited by William Toohey and William D. Thompson.

Nashville: Abingdon, 1967. 303 pp. *Volume 2, 1966-1979.* Edited by A. Duane Litfin and Haddon W. Robinson. Grand Rapids: Baker, 1983. 249 pp.

Rowley, Harold Henry. *Short Dictionary of Bible Themes.* New York: Basic Books, 1968. 114 pp.

Schuller, David S. *Ministry in America; A Report and Analysis, Based on an In-Depth Survey of 47 Denominations in the United States and Canada, with Interpretation by 18 Experts.* San Francisco: Harper & Row, 1980. 582 pp.

Spencer, Donald A., comp. *Hymn and Scripture Selection Guide; A Cross-Reference of Scripture and Hymns with Over 12,000 References for 380 Hymns and Gospel Songs.* Valley Forge, PA: Judson, 1977. 176 pp.

Von Ende, Richard C. *Church Music; An International Bibliography.* Metuchen, NJ: Scarecrow, 1980. 453 pp.

Wakefield, Gordon S., ed. *The Westminster Dictionary of Christian Spirituality.* Philadelphia: Westminster, 1983. 400 pp. Also publishes as: *A Dictionary of Christian Spirituality.*

VIII. CHRISTIAN EDUCATION; RELIGIOUS EDUCATION; AUDIO-VISUAL RESOURCES; GROUP LEADERSHIP

Annual Review of Research; Religious Education. Edited by John H. Peatling. Schenectady, NY: Character Research, 1980-- . Annual.

AVRG; Audio-Visual Resource Guide for Use in Religious Education. 9th ed. New York: Friendship, 1972.

Benson, Dennis, C., and Wolfe, Bill. *The Basic Encyclopedia for Youth Ministry.* Loveland, CO: Group Books, 1981. 351 pp.

Christian Education Catalog. Edited by Ruth G. Cheney. New York: Seabury, 1981. 186 pp.

Cully, Kendig B., ed. *The Westminster Dictionary of Christian Education.* Philadelphia: Westminster, 1963. 812 pp.

Dalglish, William A., ed. *Media for Christian Formation; A Guide to Audio-Visual Resources.* Dayton: Pflaum, 1969. 393 pp. Supplemented by: *Media Two,* 1970. 520 pp. and *Media Three,* 1973. 372 pp.

Education Index. 1929-- . New York: Wilson, 1932-- . Monthly with annual cumulations. Similar to the *Readers' Guide* but indexes education periodicals.

The Encyclopedia of Education. New York: Macmillan and

Free Press, 1971. 10 vols. *Education Yearbook*, 1973 and 1974(?).

Encyclopedia of Educational Research. Edited by Harold E. Mitzel. 5th ed. New York: Free Press, 1982. 4 vols.

Gable, Lee J., ed. *Encyclopedia for Church Group Leaders*. New York: Association Press, 1959. 633 pp.

Mental Health Materials Center, Inc. New York. *The Selective Guide to Audiovisuals for Mental Health and Family Life Education*. Edited by Jack Neher. 4th ed. Chicago: Marquis Academic Media, 1979. 511 pp.

Mental Health Materials Center, Inc. New York. *The Selective Guide to Publications for Mental Health and Family Life Eduation*. Edited by Hal Rifken. 4th ed. Chicago: Marquis Academic Media, 1979. 912 pp.

(RC) *The Resource Guide for Adult Religious Education*. Edited by Clarence W. Thomson, 2nd ed., rev. Kansas City, MO: National Catholic Reporter, 1975. 208 pp.

Taylor, Marvin J., ed. *Foundations for Christian Education in an Era of Change*. Nashville: Abingdon, 1976. 288 pp.

The Video Tape/Disc Guide: Religious Programs. Elgin, IL: David C. Cook; Long Island, NY: National Video Clearinghouse, 1981. 178 pp.

Wyckoff, Dewitte Campbell. *Bibliography in Christian Education for Seminary and College Libraries*. New York: Program Agency, Mission in Education Unit, United Presbyterian Church in the U.S.A., 1960-- . Annual. Title and publisher varies.

(E) Zuck, Roy B., and Getz, Gene A., eds. *Adult Education in the Church*. Chicago: Moody, 1970. 383 pp.

(E) Zuck, Roy B., and Clark, Robert E., eds. *Childhood Education in the Church*. Chicago: Moody, 1975. 500 pp.

(E) Zuck, Roy B., and Benson, Warren S., eds. *Youth Education in the Church*. Chicago: Moody, 1978. 478 pp.

IX. RELIGION AND PSYCHOLOGY; PSYCHOLOGY OF RELIGION; PASTORAL PSYCHOLOGY; PASTORAL COUNSELING

A. Encyclopedias, Dictionaries, and Handbooks

American Handbook of Psychiatry. Edited by Silvano Arieti. 2nd ed. New York: Basic Books, 1974. 6 vols.

Goldenson, Robert M. *The Encyclopedia of Human Behavior, Psychology, Psychiatry and Mental Health*. Garden City, NY: Doubleday, 1970. 2 vols.

International Encyclopedia of Psychiatry, Psychology, Psychoanalysis & Neurology. Edited by Benjamin B. Wolman. New York: Van Nostrand Reinhold, 1977. 12 vols. *Progress Volume*. New York: Aesculapius, 1983-- .

International Encyclopedia of the Social Sciences. Edited by David L. Sills. New York: Macmillan, 1968. 17 vols.

Oates, Wayne E., and Neely, Dirk H. *Where to Go for Help*. Rev. ed. Philadelphia: Westminster, 1972. 224 pp.

Strommen, Merton P., ed. *Research on Religious Development; A Comprehensive Handbook*. New York: Hawthorn, 1971. 904 pp.

B. Bibliographies and Book Reviews

Abstracts of Research in Pastoral Care and Counseling. Richmond, VA: National Clearing House, Joint Council on Research in Pastoral Care and Counseling, 1972-- . Annual. Entitled *Pastoral Care and Counseling Abstracts* from 1972 to 1978.

Beit-Hallahmi, Benjamin. *Psychoanalysis and Religion; A Bibliography*. Norwood, PA: Norwood, 1978. 182 pp. Limited to Freudian psychoanalysis.

Capps, Donald, and others. *Psychology of Religion; A Guide to Information Sources*. Detroit: Gale, 1976. 352 pp.

Glick, Ira D., and others. *Family Therapy and Research; An Annotated Bibliography of Articles, Books, Videotapes, and Films Published 1950-1979*. 2nd ed. New York: Grune & Stratton, 1982. 308 pp.

Horner, Tom. *Homosexuality and the Judeo-Christian Tradition; An Annotated Bibliography*. Metuchen, NJ: Scarecrow, 1981. 131 pp.

Menges, Robert J., and Dittes, James E. *Psychological Studies of Clergymen; Abstracts of Research*. New York: Nelson, 1965. 202 pp.

Miller, Albert Jay, and Acri, Michael James. *Death; A Bibliographical Guide*. Metuchen, NJ: Scarecrow, 1977. 420 pp.

Psychological Abstracts. Lancaster, PA: American Psychological Association, 1927-- . Monthly, with semiannual index.

Summerlin, Florence A., comp. *Religion and Mental Health; A Bibliography*. Rockville, MD: National Institute of Mental Health, 1980. 397 pp. Distributed by the

Government Printing Office.

X. SOCIOLOGY OF RELIGION; CHURCH AND SOCIETY

A. Encyclopedias and Handbooks

Encyclopedia of Social Work. Edited by John B. Turner. 17th ed. New York: National Association of Social Workers, 1977. 2 vols.

Fischer, Clare B. *Breaking Through; A Bibliography of Women and Religion*. Berkeley, CA: Graduate Theological Union Library, 1980. 65 pp.

International Encyclopedia of the Social Sciences. Edited by David L. Sills. New York: Macmillan, 1968. 17 vols.

Inventory of Marriage and Family Literature, 1973--. Beverly Hills, CA: Sage, 1975-- . Annual. Preceded by: *International Bibliography of Research in Marriage and the Family, 1900--1972*. 2 vols.

U.S. Bureau of the Census. *Statistical Abstract of the United States*. Washington: U.S. Government Printing Office, 1897-- . Annual.

(RC) Williams, Melvin J. *Catholic Social Thought; Its Approach to Contemporary Problems*. New York: Ronald, 1950. 567 pp. Includes a classified bibliography.

B. Bibliographies

Bauer, Gerhard, comp. *Towards a Theology of Development; An Annotated Bibliography*. Geneva: The Ecumenical Centre, 1970. 201 pp. Deals with economic and social development.

Berkowitz, Morris I., and Johnson, J. Edmund. *Social Scientific Studies of Religion; A Bibliography*. Pittsburgh: University of Pittsburgh Press, 1967. 258 pp.

Blacks in America; Bibliographic Essays, by James M. McPherson and others. Garden City, NY: Doubleday, 1971. 430 pp.

Byers, David M., and Quinn, Bernard. *Readings for Town & Country Church Workers; An Annotated Bibliography*. Washington, DC: Glenmary Research Center, 1974. 121 pp.

Fecher, Vincent John, comp. *Religion and Aging; An Annotated Bibliography*. San Antonio: Trinity University Press, 1982. 119 pp.

Goode, William J. *Social Systems and Family Patterns; A Propositional Inventory*. Indianapolis and New York:

Bobbs-Merrill, 1971. 779 pp.

Pinson, William M. *Resource Guide to Current Social Issues*. Waco, TX: Word, 1968. 272 pp.

Sociological Abstracts. New York . . . . 1953-- . Five issues per year.

Richardson, Marilyn. *Black Women and Religion; A Bibliography*. Boston: Hall, 1980. 139 pp.

Sell, Kenneth D., comp. *Divorce in the 70s; A Subject Bibliography*. Phoenix: Oryx, 1981. 191 pp.

Sociologia de la Religion y Teologia; Estudio Bibliografico/ Sociology of Religion and Theology; A Bibliography. Madrid: Editorial Cuadernos para el Dialogo, 1975. 474 pp. *Volume B*. 1978. 215 pp.

Suseelan, M.A. *Resource Book on Aging*. New York: United Church Board for Homeland Ministries, 1981. 112 pp.

U.S. Superintendent of Documents. *Monthly Catalog of United States Government Publications*. Washington: U.S. Government Printing Office, 1895-- . Monthly with annual index.

Williams, Ethel L., and Brown, Clifton L., comps. *The Howard University Bibliography of African and Afro-American Religious Studies; with Locations in American Libraries*. Wilmington, DE: Scholarly Resources, 1977. 525 pp.

XI. WORLD RELIGIONS; COMPARATIVE RELIGION

A. General

Abingdon Dictionary of Living Religions. Edited by Keith Crim. Nashville: Abingdon, 1981. 830 pp.

Adams, Charles J., ed. *A Reader's Guide to the Great Religions*. 2nd ed. New York: Free Press, 1977. 521 pp.

Berkowitz, Morris I., and Johnson, J. Edmund. *Social Scientific Studies of Religion; A Bibliography*. Pittsburgh: University of Pittsburgh Press, 1967. 258 pp.

Dictionary of Comparative Religion. Edited by S.G.F. Brandon. New York: Scribner's, 1970. 704 pp.

Diehl, Katherine Smith. *Religions, Mythologies, Folklores; An Annotated Bibliography*. 2nd ed. New York: Scarecrow, 1962. 573 pp.

al Faruqua, Isma'il R., ed. *Historical Atlas of the Religions of the World*. New York: Macmillan, 1974. 346 pp.

Karpinski, Leszek M., comp. *The Religious Life of Man; Guide to Basic Literature.* Metuchen, NJ: Scarecrow, 1978. 399 pp.

Mitros, Joseph F. *Religions; A Select Classified Bibliography.* New York: Learned, 1973. 435 pp.

A Pilgrim's Guide to Planet Earth; Traveler's Handbook & Spiritual Directory. Rev. ed. San Rafael, CA: Spiritual Community, 1981. 320 pp.

Trotti, John B., and others. *Christian Faith Amidst Pluralism; An Introductory Bibliography.* Richmond, VA: The Library, Union Theological Seminary in Virginia, 1980. 110 pp.

Zaehner, Robert Charles, ed. *The Concise Encyclopedia of Living Faiths.* 2nd ed. London: Hutchinson, 1971. 436 pp.

B. Buddhism

Hanayama, Shinsho, ed. *Shinsho Hanayama Bibliography on Buddhism.* Tokyo: Hokuseido, 1961. 869 pp.

Humphreys, Christmas. *A Popular Dictionary of Buddhism.* 2nd ed. London: Curzon, 1976. 223 pp.

Ling, T. O. *A Dictionary of Buddhism.* New York: Scribner's, 1972. 277 pp.

Reynolds, Frank E. *Guide to Buddhist Religion.* Boston: Hall, 1981. 415 pp.

Vessie, Patricia Armstrong. *Zen Buddhism; A Bibliography of Books and Articles in English, 1892-1975.* Ann Arbor: University Microfilms International, 1976. 81 pp.

Yoo, Yushin. *Books on Buddhism; An Annotated Subject Guide.* Metuchen, NJ: Scarecrow, 1973. 162 pp.

Yoo, Yushin. *Buddhism; A Subject Index to Periodical Articles in English, 1728-1971.* Metuchen, NJ: Scarecrow, 1973. 162 pp.

C. Hinduism

Dell, David J., and others. *Guide to Hindu Religion.* Boston: Hall, 1981. 461 pp.

Holland, Barron, comp. *Popular Hinduism and Hindu Mythology; An Annotated Bibliography.* Westport, CT: Greenwood, 1979. 394 pp.

Stutley, Margaret, and Stutley, James. *Harper's Dictionary of Hinduism; Its Mythology, Folklore, Philosophy, Literature, and History.* New York: Harper & Row, 1977.

372 pp.

D. Islam

Cambridge History of Islam. Edited by P.M. Holt and others. Cambridge, England: Cambridge University Press, 1970. 2 vols.

Ede, David, and others. *Guide to Islam.* Boston: Hall, 1983. 261 pp.

Encyclopedia of Islam. Edited by B. Lewis and others. Atlantic Highlands, NJ: Humanities, 1960-- . Vols. 1-5 1960-- 1978, cover "A" to "Kiraa." *Index to Volumes I-III.* 1979. 195 pp. *Supplement.* 1980-- .

Hazard, Harry W. *Atlas of Islamic History.* 3rd ed. Princeton, NJ: Princeton University Press, 1954. 49 pp.

Hughes, Thomas Patrick. *A Dictionary of Islam, Being a Cyclopaedia of the Doctrines, Rites, Ceremonies, and Customs, Together with the Technical and Theological Terms of the Muhammadan Religion.* London, 1885; Reprinted by: Clifton, NJ: Reference Book Publishers, 1965. 750 pp.

London. University. School of Oriental and African Studies. Library. *Index Islamicus, 1906-55; A Catalog of Articles on Islamic Subjects in Periodicals and Other Collective Publications.* Compiled by J.D. Pearson. Cambridge, Eng.: W. Heffer, 1958. 897 pp. *Supplements, 1956-- .* London: Mansell, 1958-- .

Penrice, John. *A Dictionary and Glossary of the Koran; With Copious Grammatical References and Explanations of the Text.* London, 1873. Reprinted by: New York: Praeger, 1971. 166 pp.

The Shorter Encyclopaedia of Islam. Edited by H.A.R. Gibb and J.K. Kramers. Ithaca, NY: Cornell University Press, 1953. 671 pp.

Zoghby, Samir M., comp. *Islam in Sub-Saharan Africa; A Partially Annotated Guide.* Washington, DC: Library of Congress, 1978. Distributed by the Government Printing Office.

E. Judaism

American Jewish Year Book. Philadelphia: Jewish Publication Society of America, 1899-- . Annual.

Bibliographical Essays in Medieval Jewish Studies; The Study of Judaism, Volume II. New York: Anti-Defamation League of B'Nai B'Rith, 1976. 392 pp.

Cutter, Charles, and Oppenheim, Micha Falk. *Jewish Ref-*

erence Sources; A Selective, Annotated Bibliographic Guide. New York: Garland, 1982. 180 pp.

Encyclopaedia Judaica. Edited by Cecil Roth and Geoffrey Wigoder. Jerusalem: Encyclopaedia Judaica, Macmillan, 1971. 16 vols.

Index to Jewish Periodicals. Cleveland: Cleveland College of Jewish Studies, 1963-- . Semiannual with annual cumulations.

The Jewish Experience in America; A Historical Bibliography. Santa Barbara, CA: ABC-Clio, 1983. 190 pp.

Kaplan, Jonathan, ed. 2000 Books and More; An Annotated and Selected Bibliography of Jewish History and Thought. Jerusalem: Magnes, 1983. 483 pp.

The New Standard Jewish Encyclopedia. Edited by Cecil Roth and Geoffrey Wigoder. Rev. ed. London: Allen, 1975. 2,028 columns.

New York Public Library, Reference Dept. Dictionary Catalog of the Jewish Collection. Boston: Hall, 1960. 14 vols. First Supplement. 1975. 8 vols.

Shunami, Shlomo. Bibliography of Jewish Bibliographies. 2nd ed. Jerusalem: Magnes Press, Hebrew University, 1969. 992 pp. Supplement, 1975. 464 pp.

The Study of Judaism; Bibliographical Essays. New York: Published for the Anti-Defamation League of B'nai B'rith by KTAV, 1972. 229 pp.

XII. ROMAN CATHOLIC CHURCH

A. Encyclopedias, Dictionaries and Handbooks

Butler, Alban. Lives of the Saints. New York: Kenedy, 1956. 4 vols.

Carlen, Mary Claudia, Sister. Dictionary of Papal Pronouncements, Leo XIII to Pius XII, 1878-1957. New York: Kenedy, 1958. 216 pp.

Catholic Almanac. Huntington, IN: Our Sunday Visitor, 1904-- . Annual.

A Catholic Dictionary of Theology; A Work Projected with the Approval of the Catholic Hierarchy of England and Wales. London: Nelson, 1962-- . Vols. 1-3, 1962-71, cover "Abandonment" to "Paradise."

Delaney, John J., and Tobin, James Edward. Dictionary of Catholic Biography. Garden City, NY: Doubleday, 1961. 1,245 pp.

Hardon, John A. Modern Catholic Dictionary. Garden City, NY: Doubleday, 1980. 635 pp.

(RC) Ministries for the Lord; A Resource Guide and Directory of Church Vocations for Men. 2nd ed. New York: Paulist, 1981. 128 pp.

New Catholic Encyclopedia. New York: McGraw-Hill, 1967. 15 vols. Supplements. 1974. 1979.

The Official Catholic Directory; For the Year of Our Lord, 1983. Skokie, IL: Kenedy, 1983. 1,490 pp. Annual.

Vatican Council (2nd: 1962-1965). The Documents of Vatican II; Introductions and Commentaries by Catholic Bishops and Experts; Responses by Protestants and Orthodox Scholars. Edited by Walter M. Abbot. New York: Guild, 1966. 794 pp.

B. Bibliographies

Catholic Periodical and Literature Index. Haverford, PA: Catholic Library Association, 1930-- . Bimonthly with two-year cumulations.

Dollen, Charles, comp. Vatican II; A Bibliography. Metuchen, NJ: Scarecrow, 1969. 208 pp.

Ellis, John Tracy, and Trisco, Robert. A Guide to American Catholic History. 2nd ed. Santa Barbara: ABC-Clio, 1982. 265 pp.

McCabe, James Patrick. Critical Guide to Catholic Reference Literature. 2nd ed. Littleton, CO: Libraries Unlimited, 1980. 282 pp.

McLean, George F., ed. An Annotated Bibliography of Philosophy in Catholic Thought, 1900-1964. New York: Ungar, 1967. 371 pp.

McLean, George F., ed. A Bibliography of Christian Philosophy and Contemporary Issues. New York: Ungar, 1967. 312 pp.

XIII. EASTERN ORTHODOX CHURCH

Andrews, Dean Timothy. The Eastern Orthodox Church; A Bibliography. 2nd ed. Brookline, MA: Holy Cross Orthodox Theological School, 1957. 79 pp.

Demetrakopoulos, George H. Dictionary of Orthodox Theology; A Summary of the Beliefs, Practices and History of the Eastern Orthodox Church. New York: Philosophical Library, 1964. 187 pp.

Kuzmission, Joe, ed. Eastern Orthodox World Directory.

Boston: Brandon, 1968. 305 pp.

Langford-James R. L1. *A Dictionary of the Eastern Ortho-dox Church*. New York: Burt Franklin, 1923. Reprinted 1976. 144 pp.

XIV. DENOMINATIONS; RELIGION IN THE U.S.

A. Encyclopedias, Dictionaries, and Handbooks

Ahlstrom, Sydney E. *A Religious History of the American People*. New Haven: Yale University Press, 1972. 1,158 pp.

Churches and Church Membership in the United States, 1980. Edited by Bernard Quinn and others. Atlanta, GA: Glenmary Research Center, 1982. 321 pp.

Mayer, Frederick Emanual. *The Religious Bodies of America*. 4th ed. St. Louis: Concordia, 1961. 598 pp. New edition in preparation.

Mead, Frank S. *Handbook of Denominations in the United States*. New 7th ed. New York: Abingdon, 1980. 300 pp.

Melton, J. Gordon. *The Encyclopedia of American Religions*. Wilmington, NC: McGrath, 1978. 2 vols.

Piepkorn, Arthur Carl. *Profiles in Belief; The Religious Bodies of the United States and Canada*. New York: Harper & Row, 1977-- . Vols. 1-4 published 1977-1979. The status of vols. 5-7 is unclear.

(E) Proctor, William. *The Born-Again Christian Catalog; A Complete Sourcebook for Evangelicals*. New York: M. Evans, 1979. 282 pp.

Religion in America, 1975– . Compiled by George H. Gallup. Princeton: Princeton Religion Research Center, 1979. Annual.

Rosten, Leo, comp. *Religions of America; Ferment and Faith in an Age of Crisis, a New Guide and Almanac*. New York: Simon and Schuster, 1975. 672 pp.

B. Bibliographies

Burr, Nelson Rollin. *A Critical Bibliography of Religion in America*. Princeton, NJ: Princeton University Press, 1961. The final two-part volume of James Ward Smith and A. Leland Jamison, eds. *Religion in American Life*. 1961-- . 4 vols. with vol. 3 forthcoming.

Burr, Nelson, comp. *Religion in American Life*. New York: Appleton-Century-Crofts, 1971. 171 pp.

(RC) Ellis, John Tracy. *A Guide to American Catholic History*. 2nd ed. Santa Barbara: ABC-Clio, 1982. 265 pp.

Hackett, David G., comp. *The New Religions; An Annotated Introductory Bibliography*. 3rd ed. Berkeley, CA: Center for the Study of New Religious Movements, 1981. 38 pp.

Jones, Charles E. *A Guide to the Study of the Holiness Movement*. Metuchen, NJ: Scarecrow, 1974. 918 pp.

Jones, Charles Edwin. *A Guide to the Study of the Pentecostal Movement*. Metuchen, NJ: Scarecrow and American Theological Library Association, 1983. 2 vols.

Religion and Society in North America; An Annotated Bibliography. Edited by Robert deV. Brunkow. Santa Barbara, CA: ABC-Clio, 1983. 515 pp.

Sandeen, Ernest R., and Hale, Frederick. *American Religion and Philosophy; A Guide to Information Sources*. Detroit: Gale, 1978. 377 pp.

Williams, Ethel L., and Brown, Clifton F., comp. *The Howard University Bibliography of African and Afro-American Religious Studies; With Locations in American Libraries*. Wilmington, DE: Scholarly Resources, 1977. 525 pp.

C. Directories

Directory of Religious Organizations in the United States. 2nd ed. Falls Church, VA: McGrath, 1982. 518 pp.

Friedlander, Ira, ed. *Year One Spiritual Directory for the New Age*. New York: Harper & Row, 1972. 152 pp.

The New Spiritual Community Guide for North America 1975-76. San Rafael, CA: Spiritual Community, 1974. 192 pp.

Yearbook of American Churches; Information on All Faiths in the U.S.A. Edited by Constant H. Jacquet, Jr. New York: National Council of Churches, 1916-- . Annual.

D. Atlas

Gausted, Edwin S. *Historical Atlas of Religion in America*. Rev. ed. New York: Harper and Row, 1976. 189 pp.

XV. ECUMENICAL MOVEMENT; ECUMENICS

Crow, Paul A. *The Ecumenical Movement in Bibliographic Outline*. New York: National Council of the Churches of Christ, 1965. 80 pp. Supplement, 1969.

De Groot, Alfred Thomas. *Church Unity; Annotated Outline of the Growth of the Ecumenical Movement*. Fort Worth: Texas Christian University, 1969. 65 pp.

Index to the World Council of Churches' Official Statements and Reports, 1948-1978. Edited by P. Beffa and others. Geneva: World Council of Churches, 1978. 104 pp.

Lescrauwaet, Josephus Franciscus. *Critical Bibliography of Ecumenical Literature*. Nijmegen, Holland: Bestelcentrale V.S.K.B., 1965. 93 pp.

Rouse, Ruth, and Neill, Stephen Charles, eds. *A History of the Ecumenical Movement*. Philadelphia: Westminster, 1967-1970. 2 vols.

World Council of Churches. *Directory of Christian Councils*. 3rd ed. Geneva: World Council of Churches, 1980. 141 pp.

World Council of Churches. Library. *Classified Catalog of the Ecumenical Movement*. Boston: Hall, 1972. 2 vols. *First Supplement*, 1981. 571 pp.

XVI. MISSIONS

A. Handbook, Dictionary, and Directory

Mission Handbook; North American Protestant Ministries Overseas. Edited by Samuel Wilson. 12th ed. Monrovia, CA: Missions Advanced Research and Communication Center, 1980.

Missions Advanced Research and Communications Center. *World Christianity*. Monrovia, CA, 1979-- . Vol. 1: Middle East. 1979. Vol. 2: Eastern Asia. 1979. Vol. 3: South Asia. 1980. Vol. 4: Central America and the Caribbean. 1981.

Neill, Stephen Charles, and others, ed. *Concise Dictionary of the Christian World Mission*. Nashville, TN: Abingdon, 1971. 682 pp.

B. Bibliographies

Anderson, Gerald H. *Bibliography of the Theology of Missions in the Twentieth Century*. 3rd ed. New York: Missionary Research Library, 1966. 119 pp.

Missionary Research Library. New York. *Dictionary Catalog*. Boston: Hall, 1968. 17 vols.

Ofori, Patrick E. *Black African Traditional Religions and Philosophy; A Select, Bibliographic Survey of the Sources from the Earliest Times to 1974*. Nendeln, Liechtenstein: Kraus-Thomson, 1975. 421 pp.

Ofori, Patrick E. *Christianity in Tropical Africa; A Selective, Annotated Bibliography*. Nendeln, Liechtenstein: KTO, 1977. 461 pp.

Sinclair, John H., ed. *Protestantism in Latin America; A Bibliographical Guide*. South Pasadena, CA: William Carey Library, 1976. 414 pp.

(RC) Streit, Robert. *Bibliotheca Missionum*. Freiburg: Herder, 1916-1974. 30 vols.

Turner, Harold W. *Bibliography of New Religious Movements in Primal Societies*. Vol. 1: *Black Africa*. Boston: Hall, 1977. 277 pp.

Vriens, Livinus. *Critical Bibliography of Missiology*. Nijmegen, Holland: Bestelcentrale der V.S.K.B., 1960. 127 pp.

Williams, Ethel L., and Brown, Clifton L., comps. *The Howard University Bibliography of African and Afro-American Religious Studies; With Locations in American Libraries*. Wilmington, DE: Scholarly Resources, 1977. 525 pp.

XVII. MYTHOLOGY AND FOLKLORE

Diehl, Katherine Smith. *Religions, Mythologies, Folklores; An Annotated Bibliography*. 2nd ed. New York: Scarecrow, 1962. 573 pp.

Frazer, James George. *The Golden Bough; A Study in Magic and Religion*. 3rd ed. 1907-15. 12 vols. Reprint. New York: St. Martin's, 1955. 13 vols. including *Aftermath*.

Funk and Wagnalls' Standard Dictionary of Folklore, Mythology and Legend. Edited by Maria Leach and Jerome Fried. New York: Funk and Wagnalls, 1949-50. 2 vols.

Grimal, Pierre, ed. *Larousse World Mythology*. New York: Putnam, 1965. 560 pp.

The Mythology of All Races. Edited by Louis Herbert Gray and George Foot Moore. 1916-32. 13 vols. Reprint. New York: Cooper Square, 1964.

Appendix 3
Guidelines for Proceeding

The questions below are designed to lead a student through a library search on a term paper topic in religion. Some questions will lead to valuable materials; others will lead to dead ends. The questions pretty much follow the chapters in this book, so if any questions need clarification, refer back to the appropriate chapter.

1. My tentative topic or topics. (Chapter 1):

2. Choosing a more precise topic.

   a. What encyclopedias, handbooks, and dictionaries listed in Appendix 2 are most useful?

   b. Is my topic interdisciplinary? If so, what encyclopedias, handbooks, and dictionaries does the reference librarian recommend?

   c. What textbooks and reserve books are most useful?

3. Narrowing the topic. (Chapter 2)

   a. What narrowing is suggested by the above encyclopedias, handbooks, dictionaries, textbooks, and reserve books?

   b. What narrowing is suggested by bibliographies? (Check those in Appendix 2 as well as those found in the card catalog under the subject subdivision, " – Bibliography." Also check with the reference librarian.)

4. Communicating with the card catalog. (Chapter 3)

   a. What subject heading(s) in the subject heading book most precisely describe my topic?

   b. What related headings are suggested by "sa" and "xx" in the subject heading books and by "see also" references in the card catalog?

   c. When I check the above headings in the card catalog, what books appear most useful?

5. Evaluating books. (Chapter 5)

   a. On what books am I basing my paper?

   b. Have they appeared on selective bibliographies?

   c. Have they been favorably reviewed? Have reviewers disagreed with any important facts or interpretations? (Check *Religion Index One: Periodicals, Book Review Digest*, and the reference librarian.)

   d. If I find no information for *b* and *c* above, do any

of the following indicate whether the author is an authority?
   Who's Who in America?
   Directory of American Scholars?
   Contemporary Authors?
   Biography Index?

6. Collecting current information. This is especially important for topics of recent controversy. (Chapter 6)

   a. What useful articles are cited in *Religion Index One: Periodicals*?

   b. In the *Catholic Periodical and Literature Index*?

   c. Is a computer search appropriate?

7. In quest of quotations. (Chapter 7)

   a. What do I find under relevant headings in *The World Treasury of Religious Quotations*?

   b. In *The Home Book of Quotations*?

8. Using guides to the literature of religion, in case my bibliography is weak. (Chapter 8)

   a. What useful sources are cited in *Reference Works for Theological Research*?

   b. In *Walford's Guide to Reference Material*?

9. Using comprehensive bibliographies, if my bibliography is still weak. (Chapter 9)

   a. What useful books are cited in *Library of Congress Catalog – Books: Subjects*?

   b. What useful books and articles are cited in the following comprehensive subject bibliographies? (Chapter 6)

      1. Bible topic: *Elenchus Bibliographicus Biblicus*?

      2. Theology topic: *Ephemerides Theologicae Lovaniensis* "Elenchus Bibliographicus"?

      3. Church history topic: *Revue d'Histoire Ecclesiastique* "Bibliographie"?

10. Using other libraries. (Chapter 9)

   a. If important books and artices are not in my library, do I have time to request interlibrary loans or photocopies?

   b. Shall I visit another library?

Index of Titles

Notes

Notes

X